BRITAIN'S
FORGOTTEN
FIGHTER ACE
Captain Albert Ball VC

BRITAIN'S FORGOTTEN FIGHTER ACE

Captain Albert Ball VC

Walter A. Briscoe and H. Russell Stannard

Foreword by
Lord Ashcroft, KCMG PC

Frontispiece: Flight Commander (Captain) Albert Ball, VC, DSO and two bars, MC, Croix de Chevalier Legion d'Honneur, Russian Order of St George.

Map: The Western Front in 1917, just prior to the Arras Offensive. Lens, where Albert Ball would be shot down, can be seen to the top left.

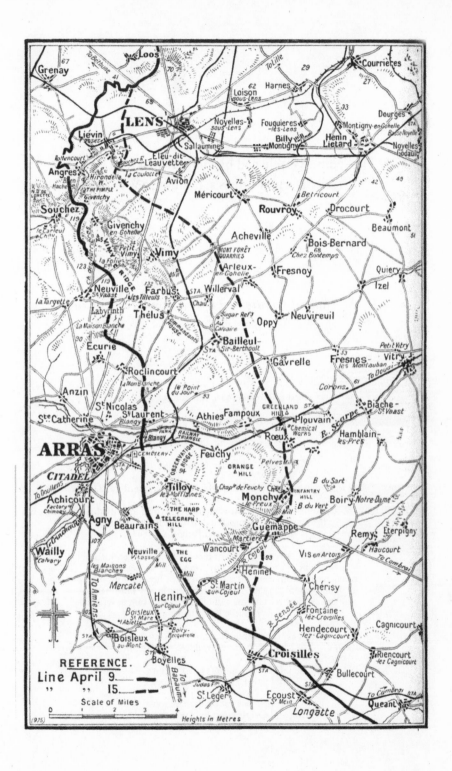

First edition published by Herbert Jenkins Limited,
3 York Street, St James's, London, SW1, 1918

To the Gallant Gentlemen of the Royal Flying Corps

First published 1918, this edition 2014

Amberley Publishing
The Hill, Stroud
Gloucestershire, GL5 4EP

www.amberley-books.com

British Library Cataloguing in Publication Data.
A catalogue record for this book is available from the British Library.

ISBN 978 1 4456 2236 1 (print)
ISBN 978 1 4456 2259 0 (ebook)

Typeset in 11pt on 15pt Sabon.
Typesetting and Origination by Amberley Publishing.
Printed in the UK.

Contents

Foreword

By Lord Ashcroft KCMG PC

My interest in bravery spans more than half a century. Over the years, it developed into a passion for gallantry medals, in general, and the Victoria Cross (VC), in particular. During the past three decades, I have been fortunate enough to build the world's largest collection of VCs (currently more than 180 in total and on public display in a gallery at Imperial War Museums, London). I have also long had a special fondness for medals awarded for courage in the air and my most recent gallantry book was entitled *Heroes of the Skies*. I find it hard to comprehend that just over a decade after man's first powered flight – performed by the Wright brothers in December 1903 – pilots were flying regularly in combat in early military aircraft as part of the Great War.

With this background in mind, I was curious when I was informed that Amberley Publishing was intending to produce a new edition of a book about one the greatest fighter pilots of the First World War, Captain Albert Ball VC, DSO & two Bars, MC. My curiosity developed into a great sense of anticipation when the publishers graciously asked if I would write the Foreword for the new edition of the book: Walter A. Briscoe and H. Russell Stannard's *Captain Ball V.C.*

I had not read the original book and, when the new edition was delivered to me, it did not disappoint – anything but. The great strength of *Captain Ball V.C.* is that it not only splendidly captures the outstanding courage of its subject but it also provides a fascinating insight into the character of the man himself. During the spring of 1917, and while serving with the Royal Flying Corps (the forerunner to the RAF), Captain Ball, the son of a Nottinghamshire alderman, repeatedly captured the public's imagination with his courage, determination and skill. These attributes led to him becoming the first man to be awarded three DSOs. On top of this, he was awarded the VC, the MC and prestigious decorations from France and Russia. His tally of forty-four official 'kills', with a further twenty-five unconfirmed, was truly remarkable as was the fact that, flying alone, he occasionally fought up to six enemy aircraft at one time. At the time of his death, he was his country's leading scoring ace and he was particularly popular with the public because of his 'lone wolf' style of combat flying, often stalking his prey from below.

It is the letters from Captain Ball to his family, coupled with numerous tributes from those who knew him well, that enables us to picture the handsome, slightly-built, modest hero. Captain Ball was a principled young man with no fondness for war and its consequences. He took no pleasure from killing enemy pilots but as he put it so succinctly in a letter to his mother: 'I only scrap because it is my duty, but I do not think anything bad about the Hun ... Nothing makes me feel more rotten than to see them go down, but you see it is either them or me, so I must do my best to make it a case of *them*.'

Time and again, Captain Ball climbed into the cockpit of his aircraft, sometimes several times a day, out of a sense of duty, and in order to serve his country and to fight for wider freedoms. When poor weather prevented pilots from flying, many felt relieved that they did not have to risk their lives confronting the enemy in the skies. It says a great deal about Captain Ball that he writes to his father about his 'rotten luck' when strong winds prevented him from flying in combat. 'No flying, so this is one day wasted,' he lamented. 'However, I think it will be right to-morrow.'

Time and again, too, Captain Ball landed his damaged aircraft and was immediately looking for another plane so that he could tackle the enemy as soon as possible.

The great sadness, of course, is that Captain Ball, like so many young pilots who flew during the Great War, never lived to receive his VC. Instead, the posthumous award was announced on 8 June 1917, a month after his aircraft crashed into a field in northern France claiming his life at the age of just 20. His parents received his decoration from King George V in an investiture at Buckingham Palace on 21 July 1917. Later his father bought the field in France where his son had died so that he could always visit the scene where Captain Ball perished. In fact, a memorial headstone was erected in the field in his honour, although his actual grave is at Annoeullin Communal Cemetery, France.

I strongly maintain that we, as a nation and as individuals, have a responsibility to remember those who have sacrificed their life fighting for their country, particularly when they have, like the gallant Captain Ball, displayed outstanding courage. I will always welcome and support books like this that champion quite astonishing bravery and that bring such noble deeds to a wider audience.

To conclude, I commend Amberley Publishing for marking the centenary of the Great War by producing a new edition of this informative, entertaining and affectionate book on one of the finest pilots that Britain has ever seen. *Captain Ball V.C.* is a labour of love: one that, nearly a century after it was written, will still be enjoyed and treasured by all who read it.

Foreword

By the Rt. Hon. D. Lloyd George MP

This war has revealed many stirring examples of heroic simplicity, but seldom have I come across so fine a spirit of devotion to freedom, home and country, as is reflected in Captain Ball's letters to his family. In all his fighting record there is no trace of resentment, revenge or cruelty. What he says in one of his letters, 'I hate this game, but it is the only thing one must do just now,' represents, I believe, the conviction of those vast armies who, realising what is at stake, have risked all and endured all that liberty may be saved.

I am sure nobody can read these letters without feeling that it is men like Captain Ball who are the true soldiers of British democracy. It is their spirit of fearless activity for the right, in their daily work, which will lead us through victory into a new world in which tyranny and oppression will have no part.
D. Lloyd George

Appreciation

By Field-Marshal Sir Douglas Haig, KT, GCB, KCIE, GCVO

By his unrivalled courage and brilliant ability as an airman, Captain Ball won for himself a pre-eminent place in a most gallant Service.

His loss was a great one; but the splendid spirit which he typified and did so much to foster lives after him.

The record of his deeds will ever stir the pride and admiration of his countrymen and act as an example and incentive to those who have taken up his work.

D. Haig, FM

An Appreciation

By Major-General Sir Hugh Trenchard, KCB, DSO (Chief of the Air Staff)

I have never met a boy who was so keen on his work, more modest, or with a greater sense of his responsibility than Ball.

The little that I could see of him made me realise that he was quite out of the ordinary; no task was too great for him to tackle and no little detail was too small for him to see to if it affected his work.

He had a wonderfully well-balanced brain, and his loss to the Flying Corps was the greatest loss it could sustain at that time.

Hugh Trenchard

My Impression of Captain Ball

By Brigadier-General J. F. A. Higgins, DSO, Royal Flying Corps, in the Field

My impression of Captain Ball was that of a very quiet, modest boy, whose only real interest in life was fighting German machines. He came out to one of my Squadrons which was doing artillery co-operation and photographic work, and I picked him out for training as a scout pilot because I thought he had the very temperament required for a single-seater fighting machine. He was by no means an exceptionally good pilot at first, but he was always practising and improving himself and he had very quick judgment in the air. One of his greatest physical qualifications as a fighting pilot was his very keen sight; he had a kind of genius for seeing German machines. He used to spend most of the time he was on the ground looking after his machine or his gun himself, and when, for any reason, his particular machine was out of action, he used to look quite miserable. He was essentially a single-handed fighter, and I am sure, preferred attacking hostile machines by himself to being one of a patrol. Although I think he was of a very highly strung temperament, he never seemed to get tired and, when I decided that he ought to be transferred home, for a period of rest, the only way I could cheer him up about it was pointing out that he might be able to bring down a Zeppelin!

Although he did not come back to my brigade when he came out again, I took a great personal interest in his achievements and I felt his loss very keenly.

J. F. A. Higgins

CHAPTER 1

The End and the Beginning

Oh, it was a good fight, and the Huns were fine sports. One tried
to ram me after I was hit and only missed by inches. I am indeed
looked after by God; but oh! I do get tired of always living to
kill, and I am really beginning to feel like a murderer. I shall be
so pleased when I have finished.

These are the words of the boy who was the first great pilot
in Britain's Air Army on the Western Front. Not until this war
is ended will it be possible to say whether or no he was the
most wonderful fighter in the air that England has produced.
Other of our incomparable young men may yet come forward
to beat his record of enemy airmen vanquished, and they may
even excel him in his individual feats over the battle lines.
But we do know that nobody can surpass him in courage and
self-sacrifice, and that whatever new and wonderful history is
to be made in the air, he will always occupy a unique position
because he flew into the Western sky at the crucial moment
when a brilliant, fearless leadership was needed.

It was his skill, example, and resource which were of incalculable
service in the months of the spring and summer of 1916 and in
the spring of 1917, when the British supremacy in the air and
its vital bearing on the campaigns of those years was never so
gravely jeopardised. Ball's invincible ardour and audacity rallied
his hard-pressed comrades in those grim days when we were short

of machines and men, and when defeat in the air would have had the gravest consequences. This simple, healthy boy who did not live to enjoy full manhood was the leader and the inspirer of those British airmen who, by their fearless work in photography, reconnaissance, observation and fighting prepared the way for the triumph of the land armies on the Somme, the Scarpe, and the Vimy Ridge, which burst through the German wall in the West.

The Ministry of Munitions has stated: 'Our command of the air is certain, but it is he who pointed out the way by fearless action, quick initiative, but always with the proper weighing of chances,' and Mr John Buchan, the historian, has said that 'all records were excelled by the British airman, Capt. Ball ... No greater marvel of skill and intrepidity has been exhibited by any service in any army, in any campaign in the history of the world.'

The spirit of young Ball, the mirthful schoolboy who found a strange joy in the new warfare, is the spirit of the young British airmen who cloud the sky to-day and pour down fire upon the German hordes.

The story of his life is essentially the story of a lad who can scarcely be described in the same terms as one would use about a mighty warrior, but rather of a young knight of gentle manners who learnt to fly and to kill at a time when all the world was killing, and who, all the time, remained a good-natured happy boy, a little saddened by the great tragedy that had come into the world and made him a terrible instrument of Death.

It is hard to think of any boy between the age of 19 and 21, who has played such a fateful part in the battle for freedom of his country. It may occur to an historian of Armageddon to dilate upon the strange Destiny which took this lad, untrained in the art of war, from his home and sent him to inflict tremendous punishment upon the most powerful and the most cruel foe civilisation has ever known.

The words which are quoted at the beginning of this chapter were written by him to his parents shortly before he was killed, and they are a true reflection of his mind and of the impression the war had made upon him. Captain Ball never once exulted over the death of an opponent. If he never sickened at the sight of death he never gloried in his power to destroy others. His letters home are the best possible record of his brief life and achievements. They are scarcely a contribution to the fine writing that has come from the trenches and also from the aerodromes in this war, but as a simple tale of what this world-famous lad thought and endured they could not be improved upon, and it is of these that this volume largely consists.

Albert Ball was fortunate in being born in the atmosphere of a prosperous home in the Midlands. He was the son of admirable parents who put in his way all the advantages of education and healthy recreation. He was born in Nottingham on 21 August 1896, one of a family of three, and the elder of two boys. His father (Alderman A. Ball, JP), an estate agent doing big business throughout the country with interests in various engineering concerns, is a prominent figure in the public life of the city, a popular Mayor in his year of office; in brief, one of the best type of energetic, enterprising business men who are assisting in the administration of the affairs of the English provincial towns.

The infant, Albert Ball, nearly put an end to his own existence at the age of 5 by setting fire to the nursery, following a successful excursion to the mantelpiece for a box of matches which he reached by way of a chair. This was the first of many adventures.

He went to Grantham Grammar School, then Nottingham High School, and finally Trent College, where it is said he arrived a 'nervy' boy, perhaps too sensitive for a public school. But he turned out well, although he did not excel in anything, his only prize being a silver cup for the obstacle race. He was keen on photography, chemistry, mechanics and gardening.

During his second term he built a boat. He had a genius for obtaining just the things he required, and he purchased the necessary materials at a nominal cost; and soon to the gratification of his fellow-tridents, the 'ark' was an accomplished fact. It was not destined to be merely a pond boat – for the mere edification of pleasure-loving juniors – but seriously intended for trips on the river. The sequel to it all was that, with willing assistance, he got it to the river, and actually sailed down from Long Eaton to Nottingham. He arrived on the canal, which may be seen from his home, right in front of his own house on his own craft, to his great satisfaction, and to the surprise of his people.

During a school vacation, part of which time was spent in Skegness, he made a raft. He secured the necessary planks and fastened them together. In the centre he fixed a pole, on the top of which he nailed a cricket 'blazer' to serve for a flag. One evening he was missing from the bungalow, and as it was getting dark, a family search party hied forth to the sands, where he had been last seen, with his raft tied to a stake. On arrival on the shore his people found a crowd of onlookers gazing seaward. There was young Albert on the raft hammering away to his heart's content, by the glow from a fire contained in a bucket, oblivious of the fact that he might soon be washed out to sea, if the old rope broke. When satisfied with his work he got off the raft and walked through the water, quite unconscious about the excitement he had caused on the beach. The next morning, to his chagrin, his raft got loose. He hurriedly took off most of his clothes and jumped in after it, for it was out some distance at that time. People on the beach shouted to him to come back, as it seemed quite impossible for him to gain his object or to even get back safely. Once he went under, and he said afterwards that he almost gave up, until he thought of his mother and home, and how they might miss him; so he made an extra special effort and eventually reached the raft. He could, however, do nothing to cause it to float inland, so he thought it best to dive off, especially as it was being carried further out. His swim homeward against the tide proved to be a difficult task, but he succeeded by dint of that perseverance, pluck and determination shown in his greater days, in reaching the shore. He was thoroughly exhausted and blue with cold and ague, and warm blankets and a hot water bottle, etc., were required to restore his circulation. Some fishermen brought the raft to shore, but, as it was at the other end of Skegness, it cost him all his pocket money to get it back, so he broke it up and thus ended the raft episode.

This was only another of his many early adventures.

He once got on board a steamer at Liverpool with the idea of seeking further adventures, but thought better of it at the last moment and came ashore and went back to school.

During the time he was at Trent College, his father, when Mayor of Nottingham, went to Calais to be present at the unveiling of the monument to Joseph Jacquard, inventor of the loom to which the textile industries of Nottingham are so much indebted. Young Ball went later to further strengthen *L'Entente Cordiale*!

The most cherished memory of Ball's schooldays now is a snapshot of him as a boy of fifteen standing in front of the armoury door of the Cadet Corps of which he was a member. Carved above the doorway is Nelson's message, 'England expects that every man will do his duty.' A wonderful memory and a wonderful prophecy!

A copy of the photograph now hangs in the Royal Aircraft Factory in the office of an old Trent College boy, who says: 'It is a better incentive to do our job than many exhortations.'

One little hobby of young Ball's was the secret manufacture of gunpowder, which was suddenly discontinued on the discovery in the boy's room by his father of a parcel labelled '117 lbs. Gunpowder'.

He was a good revolver shot and could knock down a stick at fifty yards in his back garden.

He was keenly interested in mechanics, a knowledge that stood him in such good stead in the years that were to follow.

His workshop was always the rendezvous of a number of kindred spirits interested in his mechanical hobbies, and he was never so happy as when demonstrating to them and when instructing his young friends in the intricacies of his various ingenious contrivances. At his home at Sedgley House, The Park, he constructed in premises at the rear a wireless plant, which was one of the finest wireless installations for miles around. He could transmit very long-distance messages. Anything in the line of electricity fascinated him, and as quite a young boy he could deal with electric lighting as capably as many a professional electrician.

Engines of any description were a delight to him, and he would purchase a discarded gas engine and dynamo, and soon have it in complete working order. His father recalls how Albert and several of his boy admirers arrived at the door of the house on one occasion, with a huge second-hand engine, big enough, at first sight, to propel a liner. It looked a hopeless case, but it was, after much struggling, dragged into his workshop, and it was not long ere it was working merrily away.

His genius for things mechanical developed year by year, until in his after years, he was able to offer to the British Government an aeroplane of his own design.

If he was an 'ordinary' sort of boy at school work and play, he was clearly of the opinion that he would do better when he left. A letter he wrote home during his last term is interesting. He said:

> Everything is going well with Cyril and myself. We have many good times at school, and there is always something funny going on here. I think I ought to go to camp as it is my last chance to join in any really good thing, whilst I belong to Trent. Mr. Warner said that we ought to go and do our best for the

upholding of the Corps and the school. Well, I have not got on specially well as regards knowledge, but I think I have made a slight improvement. I have a great love for my school and shall be sorry in many ways to leave, but I think that if I get into a good business I shall be spending my life in a much more profitable way and bringing the best out of myself. I shall try my level best to be a good straightforward business man, and follow to the best of my ability in my father's footsteps. I am anxious to know what I shall be when I leave, and I do hope father is looking about well. I think there is a lot of money to be made in the way of making small electric-lighting plants for country houses. Many people have invented these sets, but they are all so large and need so much looking after. I should like to be placed in a large electrical-engineering factory where they make all kinds of machinery from the dynamo to the power to drive it. I think that the place for me is where there is plenty of work and bustle, so that I can keep my mind to it and not be troubling about other things. I should like to have the chance to work my way up from the bottom and get to the top.

That is surely the kind of letter which a parent would rejoice at. It is instinct with the ambition to 'make good', a spirit which in pre-war days in England met with scant encouragement.

Constant reference to these keen business aims of his are to be found in his letters of these days, and later on when he was in the Army and was not entirely pre-occupied with the business of war. When he was 17 he bought an interest in an engineering company in Nottingham.

Meanwhile he became a Boy Scout and the commander of a Company patrol.

Then came the Great War in which he was to take his part.

Above: Captain of his boat.

Opposite page: Albert Ball at Trent College.

CHAPTER 2

Ready When Wanted

On the call for volunteers on the outbreak of war, at the age of 17, Albert Ball offered his services. He was the first to respond to a call for men at a recruiting meeting addressed by the Duke of Portland, and presided over by his uncle, the late Alderman Frederick Ball, the Mayor of Nottingham, at which time his own mother was acting as Mayoress for her bachelor brother-in-law.

Albert joined the city battalion of the Sherwood Foresters, Nottinghamshire and Derbyshire Regiment – the Robin Hood Territorial Battalion, whose famous old motto was, *Evocatus Paratus*.

Young Ball was carried along by that wave of patriotism which swept through Britain in those wonderful weeks of August 1914 when the young men felt that irresistible call to arms, and rushed impetuously to the colours, unknowing that there were not enough arms to go round, and uncomplainingly drilling without uniforms and equipment in rain and mud, and sleeping in tents sodden with water.

Ball was one of Kitchener's first 100,000, and he had the good fortune to join a battalion which was well-equipped and barracked. To him as much as to any lad who became a soldier in those days in the first flush of the new experience, before the casualties began to come through, it was a new heaven and a new earth. His early letters reflect buoyant spirits, a note of eagerness to get abroad, an impatience at the delay, and they were just like the letters received by hundreds of thousands of parents whose anxiety had not been deepened by the first stories of bloodshed.

His first experiences of army life were in his own city, where he trained in the Nottingham Forest and at the Drill Hall in Derby Road. His 'curriculum' was like that of the rest, the same old general order of things as our forefathers went through prior to Waterloo – the course of marching, rhythm, 'Left, left, I had a good home and I left,' etc. – but it stiffened young Albert, just as it stiffened Wellington's men in the years that went before.

It was not long before he was promoted; within a couple of weeks, he was a sergeant in the 2nd/7th. Later on he met a sergeant of the old army. The conversation that took place has since been related by the old soldier to Ball's parents.

> I was taking a stroll along the Boulevard [he said] when I saw your son, who looked quite a boy. I stopped and spoke to him, he was as much at ease in his khaki as I was myself. We had a bit of chaff about the medal-ribbons I was wearing, and he asked me what they were and all about them. Of course, I explained to him, and he said, 'Sergeant, some day *I* shall have medals to wear.' Little did I think at that time that in so short a time he would be such a great soldier.

Sergeant Albert Ball was inspired to apply for a commission, which he worked hard for, and which was granted to him in October 1914. He continued to be attached to the same regiment.

He went on with his military training in the South, being stationed at Bishop Stortford, Hertfordshire; Luton, St Albans, the hill-town lying ten miles SE of Luton, which owes its name to Alban, the first Christian martyr in Great Britain. It will since have added to its name the distinction for having been the training ground of Albert Ball.

Second Lieutenant Ball, at that time, had but one desire, to get out to France. With the object of getting an earlier 'move on', he transferred to the North-Midland Cyclists Corps, thinking that he would not have to wait so long before being 'drafted' across.

This eagerness to get out to the Front at the earliest possible moment is shown in a letter home, written from Bishop Stortford, dated 24 February 1915. By that time, after nearly seven months of desperate fighting and in the midst of the first terrible winter campaign, Britain was gradually awakening to the awful magnitude of the task that confronted her and her Allies. Already probably more men had been killed and maimed than in any previous war. Mons and the Marne were already great memories, the new soldiers were going out to the grim reality of trench warfare, the romance and glamour of the early days had faded. Every county in England was hearing almost daily of losses to its regiment. The tragic side was not lost on Ball, but he was getting impatient.

> I am very disappointed just now [he wrote]. I have just sent five boys to France, and I hear that they will be in the firing line on Monday. It is just my luck to be unable to go.
>
> Well, Captain Black says that I shall go with the first draft of reserves, which goes from here in a month's time. I may go before if we lose more of the men who are at the front. I watch every day the growing list of our men who are told off. It is surprising what a lot of the brave fellows are killed every day. I notice that it is mostly the best men who are killed in every case. Transport, troops, guns, etc., are rumbling past in long lines all the time. It is very interesting. Ten thousand are leaving for France to-night.

And he watched the procession with many a sigh that he was not of their number.

The call from the front was for more and more men, and it seemed he must go soon.

Writing on 8 March, from Bishop Stortford, he said: 'I have just received orders to get ready for the Reserve. I have to pack up at once and get off to Luton. This is going to be a nice, big job, but it is ripping to be doing a bit of something we know is real.'

There was an interesting personal touch added: 'I am pleased to hear that my works are going on fine. It is so nice to know that I have got so many good things to come back to. So many of the poor chaps will be no good after this job.'

A few days later he said he was not very happy, 'what with a death, etc., I have had a rough time.' Soon afterwards he was asking his father to find a job for a sergeant who was forced to take a month's leave, and did not wish to waste his time.

In his correspondence of the spring of 1915 he was writing with enthusiasm about the great sport of taking his platoon in extended order through bushes and rivers, and giving lectures on scouting to 200 men. He was making resolutions: 'I am going to work hard. I will stop smoking from to-night. Note the date. I do not intend these for idle words, but at times I shall fail. Then, dear dad, I shall want your advice. God will help and He has done.'

He spoke of a new billet as nearly as good as home ('but not quite'), of leading a night attack and dressing up in girl's clothes to elude the outpost line, and of the war not ending until he and his platoon got to France. He wrote several letters to his sister:

> Luton,
> Feb. 28th, 1915.

Dear Lol,

I have at last got a few seconds in which to write you for I have been having anything but a slack time. My men and myself have not been to bed for the last 48 hours, therefore you may guess I am feeling a bit of a crock.

It has been a great experience for me sending off all these men and taking over the Stores. It is my job to clear up and settle all bills, etc.

Well, dear, do please excuse short note, for I cannot keep from my bed any longer.

But for unconscious irony Ball never wrote anything to surpass the following:

April 28th, 1915.

Dearest Sister,

I do hope they will soon let us loose in France. I do not think they will be long. Nearly all the cyclists who went from Bishop Stortford are either killed or wounded. *It will be fine when we go.* We are expecting great things from our company.

The italics have been added.

He enthused over a deal in a motor cycle, by which he made a profit of £2, and sent home some money ready for another good investment when it turned up.

This enthusiasm over purely business matters was constantly revealed in his letters. He relates how he walked into a shop, bought a motor cycle, came out and sold it at once for 5s profit. Being in charge of a gun plant he finds 'great sport', and then talks about having 'another deal in my eye, but I must make certain before I buy'. He exults over the success with which he has handled canteen finance: 'I am just handing in my books. It was a big job, they are all straight, and I have made £20 clear profit.' It was after the previous failure of the canteen to pay expenses.

In June he was still in England, and complaining 'that every day seems like the one before,' and hoping that 'they will soon send us to do our bit at the front.'

In these days Albert Ball found time to go to church and he liked to mention the fact.

'Your remarks about my going to church make me laugh,' he wrote home, 'I always go to church, for it is quite a change to be able to think quietly for a short time, and I do like it, and miss it when I cannot go.'

CHAPTER 3

Learning to Fly

> I go in for a little flying now and find it great sport. I had a fall
> yesterday, but I soon got straight again and went up on another
> machine.

The casual reference was the first news of Ball's new ambition
that reached his home. If he had been going for a little fishing the
announcement could scarcely have been more matter-of-fact.

It was while he was in training near Ealing and at Luton that
he took the first step which was the beginning of his career; he
was destined never to fight the German on land, for he did not
go to France until he was a pilot.

Hendon was the magnet. It was a long motorcycle run from
his camp, and it meant getting up at 3 a.m. and returning in
time for 6 a.m. parade, but nothing was too much trouble for
Ball. In the first hours after dawn the weather conditions are
usually the best for flying, especially for learning to fly; it is a
maxim worth remembering that 'the man who would learn to
fly must rise with the lark'.

Ball, it seems, had not been to Hendon many times before
he made up his mind to fly. His mechanical knowledge was
a useful asset, which even some of the pioneer pilots did not
possess.

The letter in which he announced that he was flying was
written at the end of June 1915. Flying was evidently only a

side-line, for he speaks of being 'always kept hard at it' at the officers' training camp, and having very little time for writing.

Clearly the enthusiasm of a youth was formidable who, after a long and hard day's work, could rise at 3 a.m., motorcycle the 60 miles or so to London and back, take a lesson in flying and return in time to begin the 'real work of the day'.

Ball paid for his tuition. He had in fact paid £100 in fees before his father knew anything about it, and young Ball obtained his pilot's certificate at his own expense before applying for his transfer to the Royal Flying Corps.

Ball became an airman at an ideal age. He was barely 18 when he took his first lessons, and it is now generally recognised in the Royal Flying Corps that between 18 and 25 is the period when all the qualities that go to make up a valuable pilot flourish the most vigorously.

'Give me a boy of about nineteen, strong and healthy, keen on most sports – overflowing with self assurance and who thinks he knows everything,' once said a brigadier-general in the RFC. 'A boy who believes he can get anywhere and do anything – who does not know what "nerves" mean. That's the sort of fellow we want.'

It would be an exaggeration to say that in regard to candidature for the RFC, it is a case of 'too old at 25', for there have been exceptionally good pilots considerably above that age. The late Lord Lucas at the age of 40 with a cork leg, who met his death flying over the German lines, was a notable instance; but extreme youth supplies the vitality and power of the British Air Army.

The public schools of Britain have supplied a great number of pilots, and in many respects the Royal Flying Corps is the embodiment of the spirit of the British public schoolboy, with his self-confidence and audacity, courage and reverence for sportsmanship and all that it stands for in the life of the nation.

Ball was a healthy-minded public schoolboy of the best type, who had other interests besides sport. He had an American enthusiasm and delight in mechanics. A motorcycle was a thing of joy. The hum of an engine was as music in his ears. He would spend many hours tinkering with engine-parts, himself all covered with oil. He would not slack. Idle hands were a misery to him. He always wrote a cheery letter after a hard day's work, and only grumbled when he had nothing to do.

> Our C.O. sent for me this morning [he wrote] and said, 'Ball, you have got many things to learn,' He told me that I had got to come dressed in a clean uniform and not in any oily things. Well, he is giving me a chance until Monday, so I shall have to give up looking like work and go like a nut. It seems strange, but it is so, and I shall have to see that rules are carried out. All the other chaps are dressed well, so I shall have to put a clean uniform on.

Yet he was never slovenly in his dress. No youth with his self-respect and alert mind could be; but he hated to take off his working clothes, because it meant also leaving the work.

The aeroplane came to Ball as it came to thousands of other youths of England, as the apotheosis of this mechanical age. What was possible only to a few in peace time was brought within the reach of many by the war.

Within the space of a year more progress was made towards perfection in the flying machine than would probably have been accomplished in ten years in less urgent times.

Flying became to the young about as easy and as safe as motoring. It is doubtful whether it will ever be possible for the average elderly man to fly a heavier than air machine, but to the youth of the future it will be the greatest of all sports.

When Ball began great improvements had been made, but the machines then in use were still far from satisfactory and a pilot rarely had complete confidence in his engine. There were many smashes, and Ball had his share, but he was very lucky and the same good fortune smiled upon him for some time afterwards in France.

During the period of his novitiate he experienced very little fear. When at the thrilling moment he found himself for the first time alone in the air with a machine that behaved strangely and uncertainly, he only experienced an exhilaration that banished the sense of danger. There have been many men who, at that critical stage, have lost their nerve, have had a bad smash, and have never again found sufficient confidence to make another attempt. They were not born to fly.

A writer in the Press has made the interesting assertion that the expert air fighter is almost always small, trim, alert and compact, and that such a physique commonly goes with an ability to make lightning decisions. There is a good deal of truth in this, and Ball was certainly a case in point. He was quick without being erratic, and he rarely hesitated.

In the air there is no room for compromise. A moment lost in making up one's mind may be fatal.

Ball's first description of his sensations while flying was given in a letter to his father in June, 1915, when he expressed the opinion that he would make a good pilot. He said:

Well, you asked me to let you know all about my flying. I am only too pleased to let you know, for I am getting on fine. I go to Hendon every morning at 4 o'clock, and I hope to pass for my ticket in a few weeks. If I pass I get £60 back from the R.F.C. In the first place you have to pay £75. I have paid £ 10. I love flying, and as they are very short of pilots, I may do a little good. I went up the other day and got out of sight of land, and then turned straight down to earth with the tail pointing straight up. The ground seemed to rush up to meet me, and my ears and nose seemed to be bleeding, but it was ripping. I think that I shall make a good pilot. Well, I shall be able to tell you more when I get home.

His letters to his sister about this time are in a still lighter vein. Here are one or two extracts:

> Well, I am getting on ripping with my flying. I went up yesterday at 4 a.m., 100 ft. above the clouds, and it was fine. I then took a dive to the ground and landed ripping. You would love the sport, it makes your heart go into your mouth. I hope to see you before long. I shall simply love to have a good romp with you.
>
> I am on a rotten job to-night. I am orderly officer and the company has gone off until 1 o'clock, and I have to stay here until they come back, with nothing to do but sit in a wooden hut and look at the walls. However, it is a good chance to write letters.
>
> *Re* my flying, I get very few mornings in which I can go just now, for I am on duty here nearly every morning. I do hope that I shall soon get a better chance, for I am so keen.
>
> Well, my flying is going on fine, but I am very sorry to say that a great many of our men have been killed in the last few weeks. It is rotten to see the smashes. Yesterday, a ripping boy had a smash, and when we got up to him he was nearly dead, he had got a two-inch piece of wood right through his head and died this morning. If you would like a flight I should be pleased to take you any time you wish.

That last sentence is about as good an example of a schoolboy's anti-climax as one could think of!

Hendon.

Dear Lol,

I was so pleased to get your ripping cake, but I have nearly finished it. I love to take a huge piece with me when I fly.

I cannot say when I shall take my ticket. I saw a rotten smash yesterday, a boy came down 200 feet, smashed his arm in three places and nearly got burned to death. I am going on fine.

A few days previously, in a letter to his father, he had made interesting and candid comments on some of his brother officers with an incidental reference to his flying lessons. The letter is given because it shows that at this critical stage he evidently realised the importance of keeping fit, and of leading an abstemious life.

> I was so pleased to get your ripping letter, and to hear that you are well again. I am having a much better time at camp just now, for we are getting a lot more time off. I am going to the pictures for the first time since I have been at camp. It will be sport.
>
> This camp is opening my eyes very wide. One chap has been out for six nights without any sleep. He goes up to town and has a good time, as he calls it. However, some of the chaps are ripping.
>
> I had a fine time at Hendon on Sunday. The engines went wrong, and we came down in a lot of trees. However, after walking back to Hendon, I soon got up in another (machine).
>
> They say I make a ripping flyer, and I must say that I like it and find that I can do anything with the machines. It makes me laugh when you say that it is dangerous to fly, for this branch of the Army is the safest.

Those of his comrades who still survive him will smile at these words about the safest branch of the Army. If ever any man found a 'safe' job and converted it into the most dangerous of all it was Ball. Later on he went out seeking death almost daily, and when one day he was given a comparatively 'safe' post at home, he deliberately left it and flew to France to throw down the challenge again.

Ball came through his training without a broken limb, or a badly shaken nervous system. He had two bad falls, but they left him sound and whole. He makes this humorous reference to one of his escapes in a letter he wrote home when he was stationed in Norfolk:

At last I am in writing form again, I simply could not write a letter of any length yesterday. I feel rotten to-day, but just feel like writing. Well, you know by now about my smash; it was a good one. They say that I crashed to earth at 120 miles an hour, and to look at the undercarriage I should think that I did; however, it is nearly ready for flying again now. It was a rum feeling coming down, for I had time to see that my number was up; *however, it is not.*

I went up this morning for one hour at 12,000 feet. I went right over the broads and could see the sea; it was really fine. When I came down I got into a rotten row for staying up for so long and going at such a pace, but they are calm again now, and let me go up before anyone this afternoon.

Our C.O. has fixed a price per head at the hotel, etc. I think it high, but we have to do what we are told, and perhaps the C.O. thinks that if we have to spend our pay on our billet some of the chaps will not have any cash for playing the fool.

At this time many learners were being killed, or badly injured, in accidents, due generally to common causes – a sudden nose dive, a complete loss of control, faulty engines, shutting off the engine too soon when coming down, catching fire, making too steep a spiral descent, the collapse of a wing, or the tail dive due to defects in construction. Some lives were lost because of men attempting tricks which they had neither the experience nor the skill to accomplish. Ball, according to most accounts, was not in these days attempting foolhardy things, although it was not long before he was 'looping the loop'.

It was plain to his superior officers that he had exceptional skill, and that he would make a very clever pilot.

In his very next letter written two days after the one just quoted, in asking his parents to come and see him fly, he shows that he was cautious:

Now really you must come over soon, for I should so like to see you. It is not usual for parents to come to the flying ground, but do please come. I thought that I should get over this week-end, but I saw that it was going to be fine and right for flying, so I asked to be allowed to stay.

I do hope that Cyril will have good luck.[1] It would be fine if he would join the R.F.C. and come out with me as an observer. Ask him if he will. *Now he would be safe with ME.* You say that you would like to see me sitting by the fire on Sunday night. I should like to see myself, and I would give you my word you would have a lot of tales, as you say, and they would be like fairy tales; but really, mother, there is no need to make fairy tales of flying experiences, for although I do not consider it dangerous, I see more every day that it is of the greatest importance that a pilot should never attempt anything out of the ordinary, unless it is really worth the risk. Well, I had a ripping time this week-end, heaps of sport. To-day I went up in a fighting machine - it was fine. To-night I am off to the Empire with a few of the boys.

Here are some interesting extracts from letters written while he was starting on his flying career. There are references to other interests besides those of the air, and they show what a full, active, conscientious life Ball was leading, equipping himself to the best of his ability that he might serve his country well:

O. T. Camp,
July 11th, 1915.

Dear Mother,

I have just received your ripping letter, and I must say that I ought to answer it at once. Well, it is Sunday, and I have just come in from Hendon. This afternoon I am going on the river and to-night I am going to church. I shall have to get to bed about eight o'clock to-night, get up at three o'clock on Monday morning and go to Hendon, get back to Perivale in time for 6.45 parade and so on. You can guess I get plenty to do.

You will be pleased to know that in three weeks' time I hope to pass in an exam, in flying. Please do not be cross with me for flying, for it means that if the country is ever short of pilots I shall have to go.

The country became very short of pilots and Ball went at the time they were most needed.

> N.M.D.C.C., Orderly Room,
> Luton,
> July 21st.

Dear Dad,

Thanks so much for your ripping letter. It was brought by one of the officers to my camp. We slept out all last night and did our own cooking. It was great sport. We return to Luton to-day at 10 o'clock, and the men have got the remainder of to-day off; ripping for them, is it not?

I am passing the tests for my flying ticket, and I think that it will be fine.

Well, at 3 o'clock to-morrow I shall fly four miles at 75 miles an hour in a B.P. It will be fine sport. I am so looking forward to it.

> St. Alban's,
> August 3rd.

I went flying a few hours ago and had a ripping flight. I took a dive of 100 feet, and I must say I thought it was all up with me, but it got right again.

Whether the 100 feet dive was an accident or merely part of a lesson he did not explain.

St. Alban's,

August 5th.

I was up at three flying, and have also had a big day out with my platoon, finishing up again at Hendon to-night.

The last note might have been headed 'A day in the life of an officer.' At three o'clock of a summer morning he goes flying, not merely as a pleasure trip, but in the course of the anxious business of learning how to do it. Flying finished for the morning only, he scurries back on his motor cycle to St Alban's for an arduous day with the land army. Most of his brother officers in the army were probably tired out by their exertions. Not so Ball, who hops on his machine again – races off to Hendon and gets in some more flying before dark. What kind of *kultur* could implant this sort of voluntary zeal for efficiency in a lad?

Yet he found it hard to work in all his flying lessons:

St. Albans,

August 9th.

Just a short line in order to let you know how things are going. I am going on fine with my flying, but get so little time that I am finding it a big job to keep up with the lessons, but it will be better in a few days I hope.

And he wondered why he was getting 'serious' letters from home!

St. Albans,

August 10th.

Dear Dad,

Thanks so much for your ripping letter.

I received it this morning just before I went on parade.

You do make me laugh by sending such very serious letters. If I took life as serious as you do, I should be dead by to-morrow.

However, as you say, when I do think, I quite see that you only preach in order to do me good.

But Ball was really taking it very seriously. He always did in spite of his irresponsibility.

> St. Albans,
> August 12th.

Dear Dad,

I am orderly officer for to-day, so have got a few hours off.

I am having a ripping time just now, but I get very little time for flying, only about twice a week. This is no good.

> St. Albans,
> August 14th.

I do hope that we are doing our share of war work at the Works, for everyone ought to do their best.

> St. Albans,
> August 31st.

Dear Dad,

I am up to the eyes with work, and I am now really on my way with my flying. I have only half-an-hour to write this letter and four others, so I shall have to buck up.

Now I am away from here on Monday morning. I want to start at some works at 9 o'clock on Monday morning. During my stay at these works I shall fly each morning at 5 o'clock at Hendon, and take my ticket about September 10th. After I have had a week or ten days at these works here, I wish to spend two weeks at Austin's, after this my knowledge of machines ought to be very good.

P.S. – Enclosed photo of myself and machine, on which I hope to take my ticket.

Ball was determined to learn everything about the machines he was going to fly. It meant a great deal in later days when he was able to put his engine right himself in an emergency. The importance of a pilot having a thorough knowledge of his machine has been emphasised by Brigadier-General J. G. Hearson, DSO, RE, the general officer commanding the Training Division of the RFC:

> Some people thought that the larger the show the less important the individual. Never was there a greater fallacy in the Air Service. The opportunity to an individual in that service making his way was almost boundless. How had the great pilots of the war made their names? Not by luck, but by sheer hard work, by learning all the details of their profession. The pilot who did not know the details of his work was asking for trouble. He might miss a priceless opportunity in a moment through lack of knowledge, and throw away his life for the same reason.

It is safe to say that Ball never missed an opportunity through lack of knowledge.

Learning to fly in the days when Ball was training was to take your chance in a succession of smashes. He says on 15 September: 'Things are going on fair here now. We seem very unlucky at our School, for all our machines have been smashed up three times. However, they are all well again now.'

Early in October he was back again at Hendon, after a short visit to Folkestone, where the flying 'was fine'; but delays occurred before he gained his ticket.

> I have had rotten luck to-day [he laments to his father]. I waited my turn until one of our men had taken his ticket, and immediately a huge wind sprang up. It was rotten, for I could not have a flight. It is just the same to-night, 'No flying,' so this is one day wasted. However, I think it will be right to-morrow.

I have spent a little time pike fishing, but have not had a catch yet.

The next day he wrote again to his father telling of his ill luck.

You will be sorry to hear that although I got there [the flying ground] at six and stayed until eight, I got no flight, for the wind is a great deal too high. However, it seems to be going down now, so after breakfast I shall go down again. I simply must finish in a day or so. I cannot say to a flight when I shall take my ticket, but it will not be long.

We have had another smash since I sent my last letter, but the pilot was only cut in the face, but the machine was smashed up.

In his next letter to his mother, the boy is once more uppermost.

When am I going to get a letter from you? [he enquires] They do seem a long time in coming. Do please let me have a long one, with heaps of news, and a big *cake*. You make me a cake, and I would like it all the more. I so love to have a huge piece of cake to go flying with in the morning. It is fine, and if made by you would be better still.

I am having a ripping time. All our School machines are in order now. I am having a morning off to write letters, for I do not often like writing, and when I do it is best for me to get to work at once.

It is difficult to imagine a Hun airman going up with a hunk of cake in his hand; but in everything he did, Ball was half schoolboy, half soldier, but wholly lovable. In a letter to his mother and father, dated 12 September, he tells of his first experience of war. The Huns had raided a certain place in England, where he was quartered; he writes from Hendon: 'At last I am back safe and sound,' he writes, 'had a ripping time.'

Well, things are pretty rotten here. Last night we could actually see the beasts in the air, but could do nothing.[2]

I have had a quiet afternoon on the lake, it has been ripping. To-morrow I am going to church after I have been flying.

Well, I have little more to say, but I am very pleased to see the works getting on so well.

In another letter to his father he shows that most lovable combination of the inconsequent boy, and the serious-minded man so characteristic of him.

You will be pleased to know that all is well at Hendon, and the flying, etc., going fine.

I am having this morning off for the purpose of writing a few letters, for I can only write letters when I feel like it, and I feel like it just now.

I want a rod and line. Do please let me have one you do not want, for a few days, and I also want a float, etc., and a pike spoon.

I shall be off to church in the morning after I have been flying, and in the afternoon shall go fishing on the lake, and at night flying again. It seems a quiet programme for me, but it is fine.

I was so pleased to read in the papers that the Night Clubs were going to be stopped. It is a fine move. A lot of our officers have been up all last night at a Night Club. I went to see "Betty" at London, it was fine, and I got back at 12 o'clock.

If Ball had gone to night clubs the world might possibly never have heard of him. Church and fishing fortunately were much more to his taste. Combined with flying it sounds a pretty full programme, and letter-writing, as always with him, was the hardest task of all.

Notes

1. His brother, 2nd-Lieut. Cyril Ball, a pilot in the R.F.C. and now [at the time of writing, 1918] a prisoner in Germany.
2. He is referring to one of the early Zeppelin raids when our Pilots had no suitable machine for night flying.

Next page: Second Lieutenant A. Ball, photographed after obtaining his pilot's certificate.

CHAPTER 4

A Promising Pupil

He took to flying like a duck does to water. His coolness in the face of danger was most exceptional.

This is what his tutor, M. Ami Bauman, of the Ruffi-Bauman School, Hendon, said about Ball. He regarded him as one of his best pupils.

Most interesting testimony on this point has been furnished by Mr. Clarence Winchester in a valuable article in *The Daily Mail*:

As one type of pupil, I will cite Captain Ball, V.C., described as England's greatest airman.

He joined a flying school with which I was connected, and I think that I was the first person to explain aeroplane controls to him. None of us at the school expected him to become 'the complete Hun strafer.'

Of small build, with always a flushed complexion, he was excitable, and at times almost 'nervy'. Many of our pupils flew better than he did, although on taking his RFC ticket he flew very well; but he was by no means a 'star turn' among them. Yet his military flying career was one of the most brilliant on record, and I believe the secret of his success was a nervous sensitiveness usually found in artists, musicians and poets. He had 'hands' and 'felt' what he was doing in the air, just as a horseman must have 'hands' to ride well. There is no general rule as to the characteristics to be found in a good pilot, but I can safely say that to possess 'hands' - to feel part of an aeroplane that really has a temperament of its own - is very important so far as actual flying is concerned.

Mr Winchester's suggestive analysis is corroborated by the statement that at school he was a 'nervy' sensitive boy, and his simple love of gardening and of his violin showed that there was a good deal of the artist in his nature. By October he had made such good progress that he was confident he would shortly get his certificate. Writing from Hendon on 6 October he said:

> I have received a letter from my C.O., and find that I am still with the N.M.D.C.C., until I get my transfer.
>
> I shall be able to take my ticket next week, if all is well.
>
> I had a ripping flight to-night, doing six straights. Bauman says I shall get through about Tuesday.
>
> Well, Dad, I do hope you feel much better now. Please do not trouble about me for I am all right. Please give my best love to Mother.

In spite of his assurance to his parents that flying was safe, Ball in a letter to his father, dated 8 October, inadvertently shows the other side of the picture.

> I am now getting on fine. I had a ripping flight this morning at 6.30 a.m., but had a very near shave to a smash. However, I came off all right. I was nearly caught in the backwash of another machine, and it nearly turned me over. Yesterday, one of the men had a rotten smash, breaking his arm in three places, at the same time getting nearly burned to death. However, he is getting on much better to-day, and will get over it. I shall finish one day next week and will let you know.

More ill luck followed.

'It is a rotten morning this morning,' he wrote a few days later, 'so much wind that we cannot fly; however, I am staying in for the wind may drop, and there are many things to learn beside flying - Morse, map reading, use of instruments, etc.' The day he got his pilot's certificate his elation knew no bounds. Writing on 15 October, just before he passed the test, he said:

Dear Dad,
It is now Thursday morning, and through the wind blowing so much on Monday and Tuesday I have not got my ticket yet.

I did some ripping flying by myself this morning, but now the wind is up again, but I shall stay on the ground all this afternoon, and if it drops for half-an-hour I am going up for my ticket.

Lois[1] and Cyril came down, but only saw me do straights.

We went up to town yesterday, and I called at the War Office and was told that I was in the Flying Corps and should be told when to report in a few days.

I have had to send a cheque for £1 10s. in order to be in the Royal Flying Corps.

Well, please excuse short note as I am very excited.

Towards the end of October he went to Norwich.

Officers' Mess,
R.F.C.

I had my first flight in a R.F.C. machine this morning [he writes to his parents]. They were very pleased with me, and I was put in the pilot's seat at once. It is fine piloting these huge machines, after flying the old crocks at Hendon [the practice machines]. I am not in the run of things yet, but we are in a very out-of-the-way place outside Norwich and have to go by car into.

A few days later in another letter to his parents he records:

Strange things have now come to pass, for we are no longer under canvas, but are in billets. I have been sent to the Royal Hotel with twelve other fellows. Well, it is a good change after being under canvas.

You will be pleased to hear that to-day I was told to take up a machine for half an hour just when I wished; you bet I had a fine time, went up to two thousand feet and then finished by doing three good landings. I got right over—, and it was fine to look down on the people, they looked like black pins going about. I shall soon be on my third machine if all goes well, I shall then get on to Harrow Hill to finish my course.

A few days later, when still at Norwich, he had his first chance of going to France, but as an observer only, and, although the temptation was strong, he decided to wait until he could go as a pilot.

'We are having a rotten and most uninteresting time just now,' he wrote from his new training camp where he had gone to complete his education as a pilot.

The weather was Ball's chief enemy at this period. He was a serious pilot bent on learning his business, and wind and rain were to him the arch-Huns.

It rains and blows and seems as if it never will do anything else [he writes to Mr. and Mrs. Ball early in November]. I do hope that it will soon clear up, for we are doing no flying. All we get is a lecture about four times each day, the rest of the time we have to slack or read. However, we are still in hopes of the rain stopping. We have been let off early to-night, so I am writing your letter before dinner; after dinner I am off to the Pictures in order to keep from going mad, with having nothing to do.

Most of the churches are closed here on Sunday night, but I managed to find one. A few of the chaps are getting sent back on Monday for slacking and playing the fool. If I had not been a pilot I should be off to the Front on Monday, for all the observers are going out with No. 18. If I wish to go I can give up my pilot's job and go as an observer a month on Monday. It really is a great temptation, but I think as I had paid for my course at Hendon, etc., I had better wait and go as a pilot. If it was not for the thought that you might think me on my usual changing ways, I should go with No. 18 as an observer, for I really feel that I must get out.

A sign of the times that in 'the city of churches' that difficulty should be found in discovering one wherein evening service was being held.

An insight into Ball's amazing coolness is given in a letter to his sister, who had expressed fears for his safety. It shows that while he was not a reckless dare-devil, and did not throw caution to the winds, he was unflinching in the gravest emergency, and could even find humour when only tragedy seemed imminent:

> Please do not send me any more letters saying that I shall have a crash, or words to that effect. I did not think of your letter when I went up this morning, but when I got up 800 feet and had only done one circuit, my control went wrong, and I came crashing down, smashing the bottom of the machine in. I was not hurt, but it made me think of your letter. Well, it was really rotten to have a smash, for I was the first to go up for over a week now. It has been raining so much that the beginners have not been able to fly. However, the C.O. said that it was not my fault, so I am none the worse for it.
>
> You really would be surprised if you were in a smash. I just felt ripping; I had heaps of time to think what was taking place, in fact it made me laugh, although I thought it rotten to smash the machine. The air rushed past my face at an ever-increasing pace, the earth rushed up to meet me, and then crash went the

lot, and when I realised that the earth was reached, I got out of my box, walked round the machine, and after this had the machine carted on a trailer to the shed. It will be mended again by tomorrow night, so on Sunday I am going for a long cross-country flight, and am going to try and get up to 12,000 feet, for I have not been up high yet.

Now, please do not bother yourself, dear, for flying is not so bad as it looks, and really is not very dangerous.

I am having one of the broken struts sent on to you for a keepsake, also as a reminder not to send such letters, for they bring bad luck.

Seldom has a letter of reassurance been framed in less reassuring language. To send a portion of a broken aeroplane to show how safe it all was is characteristic of Ball. If anyone had pointed out to him this trifling inconsistency, he would have been the first to shout his laughter and cry, 'Ripping!'

It was November, and the weather was typical of the month. There were many wet days, and, therefore, no flying, and Albert Ball had nothing to do and consequently was miserable.

He speaks of getting in a flight one day when the weather was bad and nobody else was allowed to go up, and he tells how he has been made 'master of two machines – the Caudron and the Morris L.H.'

The lowest note of despondency was reached on the last day of the month, when he said: 'Really, things are rotten just now. No flying and no work of any kind. I have had a row at my billet and told them I should leave, and I think I shall.'

Then two days later he wrote a really delightful letter relating the ups and downs (temperamentally) of a flying man.

Am now on my long and rotten duty of Orderly Officer. However, I have only got nine hours more, and am then free from the job for three weeks. Well, to-day has been full of joys.

Flying for me has been perfect, and I have had a real good time. I went down to my billet in the C.O.'s tender this morning in order to get a shave and a wash, for after being on all night you need a wash. I then went back to camp, turned out the guard, etc., and after these few duties I was sent for from the flying ground. I arrived at the flying ground never expecting a flight. However, my instructor came along and told me to take up a machine solo. You bet I nearly went mad, I was so pleased.

I got up 300 ft., and did a landing. It was a rotten landing, and I was not at all pleased with myself, nor was my instructor. He came up, told me to get out, and advised me to look for a good flying school for girls and join it at once. He ended up with saying he would never let me fly again. You may guess by this time I was getting a little ratty, and at last I told him a few things. I told him that as I had only had 15 minutes' instruction of the S.H., he could not expect me to even fly them, let alone learn them, and I ended up by saying that if I could not fly, and he would not let me use the machine, the best thing to do was to get back to the N.M.D.C.C., for I have no time to spend watching other people fly.

He at once got another machine out and told me to get off on it. I did so, and made five perfect landings. He was very pleased with me, and you bet I was very pleased with myself.

So now I am master of No. 3 machine, and with a bit of luck shall soon be getting off to another flying ground.

Well, I am always so pleased when we have had a good day for flying, for it really makes such a huge difference if you can mix a little pleasure with the work.

I am already picking up my violin very quickly, and shall soon be able to play it again.

Ball had now reached the stage when he had sufficient confidence to practice some tricky flying. His first performance caused something of a sensation:

December 5th.

Although it has not exactly been fine for flying, I have been allowed to do a great deal of work. I started my day of success by flying for half an hour in the clouds. Well, as you know, when in the clouds you cannot see land, or even sky. However, I stuck to the machine and flew it right through the clouds. I then did a right hand spiral, and landed most rippingly in the middle of the flying ground. Well, this surprised the officers, and I think it more than surprised the Instructor. However, the afternoon came and I was told to go up first. The clouds were not very low in the afternoon, so I was able to get up high and still see land. So I went up fifteen hundred feet, put the nose down and did a left hand spiral, finishing up with a perfect landing. Of course, everyone came rushing up at once, expecting to hear me told off by the Instructor, for spirals by pupils are not allowed. However, all he said was: 'In the future when you wish to try any tricks, get well clear of the flying ground, and for God's sake be careful.'

The chaps could not believe their ears, but this was not the end, for before I left the ground Captain Cox came up and told me next week I could have a flight in his 80 h.p. machine. I was also told that if I wished I could go to another flying-ground and learn to fly the very fast English fighting machines, so I look like having a lot of good sport.

Really, you cannot guess how I love flying, and how anxious I am to get on.

P.S. – I tried to find a church to-night, but they are nearly all closed on account of not being able to show lights.

These days of December were a sheer delight to the young airman. 'I am so happy that I can only just guide the pen along the paper,' he wrote home. Before the New Year he had left the Eastern Counties to go south to the Flying school at Upavon. Two letters he wrote before he changed his quarters must be given. They show that he was itching to get out to France.

December 9th.

To-day has been a very heavy day for me. I have flown three times, and the last time I had to fly in the wind and rain. It was a big strain for I got a lot of very bad bumps. One bump dropped my machine 300 feet. However, I was up 3,000 feet, so was able to recover long before I reached the ground. Another bump turned my machine right round, at the same time dropping twelve feet. I really did think that all was up then, for I was only 300 feet up. However, I did not crash, but it was not nice and really was a big strain, but one must take a few risks in order to become a good pilot. I managed to do three spirals, although the wind was very high.

I am so pleased my works are going well, and I do hope that, as you say, I shall come home fit and well and work hard at my work. But one job at a time is enough for a boy of my age, and I shall have to try and do my bit here first. I shall go mad on the day I fly out for the front. I simply long to have a smack, but my turn is really a long time coming.

Well, I am some violin player now. I have a whack at it every night, so you bet I am making big strides.

Norwich,
December 12th.

Getting on fine, and shall be off to another camp next week. I got up this morning about 8.30, for it is Sunday and we do not fly until 10 o'clock. However, it was snowing so hard that I thought it was all up with the flying question, so I got ready for church, as soon as I was ready it cleared up, so to flying I had to go.

I had a ripping flight over Norwich, and did a spiral round the church tower. I could just hear the bells ringing, but my engine drowned the sound. It was very nice over the town at 3,000 feet, so I had a good run. This afternoon I went up to the flying ground, but there were no machines out, so I walked back, and here I am trying to write you a letter.

Well, I must switch off the ink supply now, for I am off to find a church.

Christmas he spent away from home, going to the Central Flying School at Upavon. To his brother and sister he wrote:

> Central Flying School,
> Upavon, Wilts.
> Dec. 28th, 1915.
>
> Dearest Love Lumps,
>
> Thank you so very much for the Christmas gifts. Oh, it was nice to get so many ripping things. I had twenty-seven letters and twelve Christmas boxes, and I nearly went mad.
>
> I am spending to-night writing letters. Well, you dear old things, do please excuse my short note, for I must try and thank all.
>
> Heaps of love,
>
> Your loving Brother.

After Christmas a week of rain in the south was very depressing. One weekend – the first of the New Year – his spirits rose slightly at the possibility of a little excitement and danger. He was Emergency Officer, and he was on duty in a shed ready in case of a Zeppelin raid. 'But,' he laments, 'there is never any luck for me in this way, for I never get a chance to see a Zepp here.'

So the airman turns to his violin and requests the despatch of 'one set of violin strings, two bridges, one stick of resin'.

The bad weather continued and he tried to fill up the time with lecturing and football.

But the hour was drawing rapidly near when Ball would go to war. Before he went he had his second bad smash, and it seemed that it was only by a miracle that he survived. He fully realised what a terribly narrow shave it was, but he was more sorry for his machine than himself.

You had need to wish me well with my work [he said]. I have all the luck for a short time, then everything comes down about my ears. I was getting on fine up to Saturday morning, and was really thinking a lot of things, for I had got in front of the chaps in my flight, and some of them have been here four months, trying to pass out. I was told to go off with a machine, and did so and landed quite all right. I was then told to go off again, I did so and was thrown down 1,000 feet. The machine was smashed into match-wood. Oh, and it was such a ripper. I would much rather have smashed myself than any part of the machine. However, as usual, I was not hurt at all. I came round in a few seconds and had not got a scratch, but I was so upset when I saw the machine. It was a bad day for everyone, for four other machines were smashed but only one pilot was really hurt, and he will not get over it. However, I must try to get over it and have another smack, but it has not pleased me at all.

In another reference to this bad accident he wrote:

Now you want to hear about my accident. Well, there is very little to tell. I was sent up in a big wind; a side-wind caught me as I was coming down which at once dashed the machine to earth. Everything was smashed but me. We had two other smashes on Friday, but the pilots will be all right in about six weeks. It has been a month of bad luck for all flights up to now, for twelve of our latest machines have been smashed. However, we always hope for better luck.

At week-ends we are given Sunday leave, and if we cannot fly on Saturday we are allowed to go at 12 o'clock on Saturday. I am staying at the camp this week-end, but never again. It is just about sending me mad, nothing to do and no-one to talk to. You see, Dad, we are not even near a town, in fact there is nothing to do.

Your Army is getting on fine, and I shall be most pleased to hear about your meeting. Well, Dad, it is so good of you to be looking after things for me at my works. Now I have finished answering your letter, so I will say a few words about life at Upavon. I did a lot of flying on Friday and had a good time. To-day all the officers and most of the men are away. Oh, it is rotten. I shall not stop again; however, I shall make the best of my time and write up all my notes. This afternoon I went a long walk round the flying ground. I did this so that I could look out for the best landing spots.

Before he left England he had to pass a final examination to get his 'wings', and he wasted no time, spending many hours in the workshop as well as in the air, devoting his week-ends to work.

His whole being was now entirely absorbed in this business of flying. 'Am delighted to hear that my works are still going strong,' he wrote to his father concerning a business of his own in Nottingham, 'but you must excuse me if I do not seem keen enough on my works, for it is hard to be keen on two things like flying and the works. I am very keen but really cannot take an active interest in it until I return when I shall work hard, I hope.'

On 22 January he was again at Upavon for the weekend, and was very contented. To his 'dear mother and dad' he wrote:

I have just come back from a cross-country flight. I had to make a forced landing for my machine went wrong. However, I managed to put it right, and, with the help of the villagers at Colne, got off again.

When I arrived back, and handed in my report, my C.O. said that I was to go in for my Final, either this week or next, so I shall soon be off.

I shall visit home before I go, for it may be one or even two years before I get back again.

The tenders have just left, taking all the officers 'but four' away on their leave. We have just had another bad crash. The pilot lost his head when up 1,500 ft., so you bet it has been a good smash. I have now only got two weeks workshops before I am allowed to go in for my final, so I think that at the end of about three weeks I shall go through. The Flight C.O. says that my flying is A1, but I do want to be good with engines so I shall put another two weeks in the workshops.

If I go in for my wings in three weeks, I shall be out at the front in four, so you bet if I think I am right at the end of the two weeks workshops, I shall lose no time in having a smack. The week-end I hope to spend in this way. During the afternoon I shall look over my notes in the workshops. To-night I shall walk to Upavon.

I am flying over to see Cyril in a few days, so on the way back I shall fly over the house but I shall be unable to land for there is not ground on which I could land.

I cannot play my violin now for my E string is smashed. Could you send me a black tie; I want one for my evening things. Please do not send a large one, I want one of those tiny short ones.

As it will not be long before I really go *at last*, I have decided to stay at the camp during week-ends, but it is rotten. However, it gives me a chance to go to church, also to read my notes.

You say you hope I have had a good flying in the last days. Well, it has been topping. I was flying in the rain at 7,000 ft. this morning with a 60 mile wind blowing. This made my speed only 20 miles an hour against the wind, but a good 100 down wind. Oh! it was fine; I love flying when things are not exactly A1.

On 25 January he wrote to his father: 'Am now working with full steam on, for my Final will be either to-morrow or Wednesday. Now, I did not expect to pass through until next month, so naturally I have no cash for moving, etc.'

The longed for event came unexpectedly; for on the following day his parents received the following wire: 'Have got wings, also three days' leave. Albert.'

And in the train of the telegram of express report followed Albert Ball, pilot in the RFC.

After his leave he went to Gosport as an instructor. On 4 February he wrote:

> Well, I do not know what you thought of my very short letter which I sent yesterday, but it was all I could do, so you must be satisfied. I will tell you what I have done this morning.
>
> First of all at nine o'clock I took up a Martinside for thirty minutes, I then went to the M.O. and was innoculated and vaccinated. This makes the second time since I joined the Army, so I should be alright.
>
> I went over to the flying ground afterwards and took Captain Leigh up for thirty-five minutes. He is one of the officers with me for instruction. This afternoon I am flying over to Dunnose, but I shall come back to-night. It is fine flying over the sea. On Saturday I am instructing all day on Avros, so you can see I have heaps to do.
>
> As regards getting away, I may go any day, but things do go in a strange way in the R.F.C.
>
> The place we live in here is a rotten one, about as dirty as possible. However, it is good sport.
>
> If you are making any cakes, please do not forget that I can still eat them, and shall only be too pleased to do so.

Two days later he excitedly announced to Mr. and Mrs. Ball that his novitiate was finished.

> At last [he wrote], the sport is going to commence. I have just been told by the C.O. that I am next for the E.F. so that in a few days I shall be flying in France.
>
> Yesterday I worked very hard. I was up at the flying ground at eight a.m., and did not get out until six p.m. Altogether I took thirty officers up for instruction, and out of the thirty I got six off solo.

It is good sport instructing, but out of eight officers with their wings only three of us instruct.

To-day I am Zepp officer, and have a machine that will fly 124 m.p.h., so you bet if a Zepp comes I shall have heaps of sport.

I fly from seven until nine to-night. If I had not this job, I should have gone to church. However, one cannot do all things.

On 17 February he was in London sending a farewell letter to his 'Dearest people.'

Just a line and only a line for I have only seconds on hand. I go to Boulogne by boat to-day, from there I get my machine and fly to the front. It is strange to be leaving your home on such a mad job, but cheer-oh, you dears, I shall soon be back. Good-bye.

Notes

1. His sister.

CHAPTER 5

'The Eyes of an Army'

On 17 February 1916, above a certain town on the coast of France a humming bird was heard and seen flying fast towards the east for the battle lines of Flanders. The few people who happened to give a glance at the tiny blot in the sky could not know that they were witnessing a wonderful event – as strange as if the black speck had really been a humming bird from the tropics. It was Albert Ball going to war – an 'unknown British airman' about to take his place in the fighting ranks in the air, and destined to exercise a profound influence on the course of the warfare before the summer of 1916 was out.

If the Germans could have realised what a terrible portent for them was the fast-moving object in the heavens, the anti-aircraft gunners would surely have devoted more attention to it than they did, and the German airmen might have made a special effort to end its career there and then.

As a matter of fact, the Germans had reason for a little elation about this time regarding their conduct of the campaign in the air. The temporary success of the Fokker had aroused some disquieting doubts in England as to whether or not we had lost the ascendancy which was clearly held by us during the summer and autumn of 1915. The advent of the Fokker witnessed a change; our losses became greater than the enemy's, and although the Germans never really wrested the supremacy from us, the issue hung in the balance for many weeks until new and better British machines made their appearance and began to take a heavy toll of the Fokkers.

It was an anxious time when Ball went out. Our machines were more numerous and continually over the enemy's lines, steadily 'spotting' for our guns, minutely photographing the German defences, and systematically bombing ammunition dumps and railway centres far behind the front trenches, whereas even when the Fokker was at the zenith of its power, the German excursions over our lines were much rarer and much less ambitious. But our machines were paying a heavy price for their courage and enterprise.

Flying at greater altitudes, and moving faster than our fastest machines, the Fokkers hovered like birds of prey, waiting for favourable opportunities to dive down and destroy our slow moving machines, which went on bravely with their allotted tasks, although contest was unequal and the odds heavily against them. Exposed to heavy fire from below and sudden attack from deadly foes above, these heroic airmen accomplished the work they set out to do – work which was of vital importance in the elaborate preparations that were being made for the battles of the Somme.

Ball had not, of course, sufficient experience at this time to plunge straight into the hurly-burly as a fighting airman. His early work was confined to artillery spotting, and he found it 'great sport.' That was the expression he was continually using, from the very first day of his arrival in France. To Ball and to his comrades in the Flying Corps, it was really great sport.

It was an attitude of mind which astonished the Germans. Baron Richthofen, the champion of the German Air Service, has put it on record that the English airmen do not take their work seriously but merely as so much sport. This apparent irresponsibility of their opponents puzzled and annoyed the Germans. For these young Englishmen to come along and make a circus of this sacred business of war of which, of course, the Germans were the divinely inspired protagonists, was an insult to the dignity and majesty of the German war god. How dare these English boys make fun of an art in which the German was the supreme past-master?

But what was more exasperating was that the English boys were more often the victors.

'At last we are in for the sport, and really we look like having plenty of it,' wrote Ball the day after he got to France.

> I had a nine hours' train ride last night, and am in for something to-night. The machine I am flying is a —, so I do not consider my luck very good. However, I shall have a good smack. We are now in an hotel, and a very dirty one, too; in fact, all is dirty at this place, but it is good to have a sleep at last. Oh, I can see heaps of sport ahead, but it really is mad sport.
>
> P.S. – Tell Cyril to buck up and get out, for it is great sport.

Six days later, he was over the Hun lines, and he had some rather surprising adventures.

> I am now billetted in a hut [he says] and it is very cold, as for the past two days it has been snowing hard, and even now it is coming down fairly fast. However, it is good sport.
>
> Well, I will try to tell you what has taken place in the last four days.
>
> On Sunday last we moved to a new flying ground, and I had to fly one of the machines. We spent the remainder of the day getting things in order.
>
> On Monday I was sent on some work over the Hun lines. Oh, it was sport. The Archie guns were firing at us all the time, but we were not hit; but I am sorry to say that one of our flight machines was hit and brought down by a Fokker machine. The pilot and observer were killed.
>
> On the way back from the lines my engine went wrong and I had to land. I spent nearly all night with the machine, but got

it right in the end, and started back at eight a.m. on Tuesday. It started to snow, and I could not see a thing, so I had to land. Each time the snow stopped I started up and flew a few miles, and in the end arrived back at 4.15. The Major was very pleased, for he did not expect me to bring the machine back in the snow.

There are still two of our machines out yet, and we shall soon not expect to see them again.

To-day we can do nothing but work on our machines, for the snow is too thick.

The Mess out here is run in Flights, and we have to fit up our own mess. About every three days a parcel is received by one of the officers, and we share this up with each other. The things we want are butter, cheese, jam, cake, etc., for we cannot get what we want out here. The nearest town is ten kilometres away, and the tender only goes there about once a week. Papers, etc., are also very well received.

The guns are firing all day long, and really make a beastly row.

Albert Ball can now be left to his own story of the remainder of this chapter of his early experiences in air-warfare. He was learning much and training himself for the great fights that were coming. In some respects his letters are like those of the other young airmen going through a similar course, but it is doubtful whether many of his comrades gave such delightfully ingenuous revelations of what they felt and thought about this 'great sport.' There is one passage which must be taken from its context because it gives better than anything else an impression of his boyish ardour and high spirits. Writing to his mother he says:

What do you mean by saying that when I come back I shall be a wiser and sadder boy or man? I may be wiser, but I hope that I shall have no reason to be sadder. Also there is no need for the '*boy* or *man*,' for I went a boy, and I shall return a boy, not a man. You next say that I shall have lost my boyhood. *Oh! Shall I?* I don't think. I am younger every day, and it will take many years for me to lose my boyhood.

This afternoon, Lieutenant V. and myself were playing like kids, pulling each other's hair and throwing mud at each other, also jumping on hats, etc. Why, mother, I shall always be a boy, and I like it.

Well, dear, I must really close now for supper is on the table.

P.S. – The beef and kidney puddings are first-class.

Those who met him on the several occasions he was at home on leave can testify that he never grew up, and that he never lost his boyhood.

The ruin and desolation in the French towns deeply impressed Ball, who saw them from above as well as from the ground.

We have just been to a big town just behind the lines [he wrote in April]. Oh! it was fine. It is one of the largest towns in France, but every church and house is shelled. We went into one small church and took a huge flag. When I say we went in, I mean we walked over the ruins. I gave Lieutenant V. the flag, but I have got a big band off the top. We next went into a big house. All the beds, etc., were thrown into the street, and three of the walls were down. Next we went into a huge church, one of the largest I have ever seen. Really, it was enough to make one boil with rage. The walls were done in and everything crashed up. After this we had to clear out, for the Huns had started again, and shells were coming in by the dozen. I found it most interesting, but very sad, for it is a sad thing to see such places brought down to the ground.

We have had two slack days on account of the clouds, which are only 1,000 feet up, but I think it will be clear to-morrow. Now re your letter, I am delighted to hear that you are keeping so well. Oh! it is topping. Do please always keep young.

On another day he said: 'Yesterday I went over a few big towns near the lines. It was really enough to make you sick with rage. Huge towns nothing but a heap of bricks, and churches, etc., are the same. It is a sight for the gods.'

The following are from letters written between February and June, 1916, when he got his first leave home, including some interesting details about his life, written to his sister:

February, 1916.

Hello, dear Lol,

At last a letter from good old England. Oh! you cannot guess how pleased I am to hear from home. However, time flies out here, for we have got heaps of work to do.

To-morrow I am going on a bombing patrol. It will be great sport, for the dear old Huns always shoot a lot when you go over their lines, but they do not often hit us.

The snow here is now a foot deep, but I have got a stove in my hut now, so I am all right.

Firing has not been on very much to-day, but yesterday it was like thunder. It is most interesting out here, especially going round the batteries. You see we range all the big guns from the air, and signal hits, etc., so at night we have to visit the C.O. of the batteries, and arrange about the next day's work.

Must close now for I am O. Pilot to-night.

At the beginning of March snow stopped flying, and the airmen went snowballing.

March 3rd, 1916.

Dear Lol,

I have now got time to answer your topping letter. The reason I have so much time on hand is because the snow is again coming down in lumps, to such an extent that we really cannot fly. You bet it is rotten. All our things are packed ready for the move, but we cannot get off because the tenders, etc., cannot get along the roads. Even if the roads were good we cannot fly, for we cannot see in the snow. However, all will end before long, and we shall then get a chance to move.

Well, I suppose it is no good me telling you what is taking place, for you will read in mother's and dad's letters. One thing I will tell you is: this morning we were snow-balling, and we were attacked by one of the other Flight. All our chairs and tables were smashed, and every window was smashed, so you bet it is very nice sitting here writing letters. Well, now I have some artillery work to do, so I must finish your letter later.

(6.15). Artillery is put off, so I can go on with the good work. Since I left off I have had tea, and a very good tea too, for the cake from home has just arrived, and it has also just gone, for there is nothing left now.

The snow has now finished coming down, so we may get off to-morrow. How is your horse getting on? I do quite a lot of riding in my spare time, for we are supplied with horses in order that we may take a little exercise.

After I have finished this letter, I have to unpack my bed. Heaps of love.

Previously he had an exciting day on patrol work.

February 27th.
Yesterday we were supposed to go 6n a bombing raid, but that was put off on account of the snow. However, we did some good work in the way of patrols.

To-day I was sent on the eleven o'clock artillery patrol. I started out at 10.50 with my observer. When we got up we found that the clouds were so low that we had to keep at 2,000 feet in order to see the trenches. This was rather rotten, for patrol work should be done at seven or eight thousand feet. Well, all went well until 12.5. At this point we suddenly heard a lot of

71

spluttering, and on looking down saw that we were well over the Hun lines, and they were shooting for all they were worth.

At 12.45 we started back, and when the machine was examined by the rigger, he found that it had only been hit once. I think we got off very well, don't you?

To-morrow if it is fine we shall go on the bombing raid. If not fine, we shall do patrol work over the lines … Well, I have nothing more of real interest to tell, you, so I will go on with everyday things. We have now got our mess in fine form, for we have at last got a good fireplace, and heaps of coal. I have also managed to get a stove for my hut, so we are getting on fine.

Between work we have had some fine snowballing, but I think the snow is going now.

Oh! it is sweet of you to get photos taken of me when I was a baby, but you need not stock the house with photos ready for when I have gone West, for I am not going West! Yes, I shall be very pleased to see you over here one day, but I am afraid that you will have to come on a bad day if you wish to find me in, for we are nearly always out. Well, now you must forgive me answering your letter in so short a way, but I must go to sleep now.

His first meeting with a Fokker was not fortunate. His observer's gun jammed and so did the pilot's revolver. He described the incident in a letter written on 3 March.

In the last two or three days I have had one or two near shaves. The day, before yesterday I was five miles over the Hun lines on a patrol to inspect a station and report on the trains. I got there all right, but on the way back I had a rotten time. The Archie guns shot at us from three sides, and to make it worse the old fools sent rockets up to try and set my machine on fire. We had got nearly over the lines when a Hun Fokker attacked us. My observer let fly with the gun, but after two shots the beastly thing went whonkey. I then pulled out my revolver, but this also stuck. However, by this time we were over our own lines, and the Fokker did a bunk. The rotten part about this is that if our guns had not gone whonkey, we should have had a good scrap, but, as luck would have it, things were not as I would wish. Yesterday we had a good time. I was escort to photographer over the Hun lines. We were shot at all the time, but luck was good, and we got home safely after taking all the photos of the Hun's positions we wanted.

To-day I started up and my engine went poo-poo. I managed to land my machine A1, but it was not nice, for the landing ground is full of shell holes. We are leaving this place on Saturday and going to a better place nearer the lines.

Now I will answer Mother's letter. Oh! you dear, it is good of you to send me such ripping long letters. You cannot guess how we long for letters out there, and how ripping it is when we get them. It is A1 of you to have sent cakes, etc., out for me, but I am afraid that it will be a long time before I get them for all parcels have been stopped for a few days. However, all will be well in the end, and we shall have a fine tuck in.

Now for Dad. Now, what do you mean by being whonkey for so long? Really you will have to buck up, for it puts the wind up me to keep hearing of you being in bed. Now, buck up and get well. Well, do please excuse me writing more for I must now get on the 4 o'clock patrol over the Hun lines.

One day he flew so low over the enemy lines that he could see the faces of the Huns.

March 8th.
Have only just got up, for I have nothing to do until 12 p.m. At 12 p.m. I am going over the Hun lines for a few hours. It should be good sport, for there are quite a lot of Hun machines about here. We arrived at this place on Sunday, but expect to get off

again next Sunday. It is very beastly changing places every few days, but we are waiting for a new flying-ground being finished. When it is finished we shall have a good ground, so we shall not have far to go before we get to work.

On Sunday when we arrived here we had to find our billets, and we found them. Five of us slept in a shed next to a public house, and really I have never been in such a hole. In the morning we went round the village trying to find better places. I went to a storeshop and managed in about two hours to explain that I wanted to have a 'chambre à un lit.' After a long talk we managed things, and I got a room with a bed in it. When I come to bed at night I have to pass through three other rooms in which the people of the house sleep. It is not exactly a clean place, but it is much better than the shed.

Well, you will now want to know what things we have been doing since Sunday. We have had heaps of work to do, and very interesting it was. Monday I was on a long patrol 30 miles over the Hun lines. They shot at us a great deal, but we were not hit. They also sent three Hun machines after us, but they ran off as soon as we turned towards them.

I went so low over the Hun lines that I could see their faces, but they did not hit me or even my machine. The lines at this place are only about ten yards apart, and we just fly down the centre of No Man's Land, and we can then observe what each side is doing. Yesterday I saw three trenches blown up!

To-day I hope to do a bit of good work. I am going over the lines to report on the trains, etc., in a few Hun stations. The observer I am taking is a good man. Tomorrow we are taking 36 machines about 50 miles over the lines, each machine will carry 206 lb. bombs, so I think that we shall make a few of the poor old things fly, without the help of a machine.

It is interesting to note that nothing so depressed Ball as idleness. Snow, wind and rain he regarded as his arch-enemies, because they were obstacles to flying. Time after time he complains of inactivity owing to weather conditions, just as a school-boy might gloomily regard a rain-soaked cricket pitch. He lived always in the present, the life was 'rotten' or 'topping,' according to the weather conditions. His depression, however, was that of a happy natured child, easily turned into a laugh or smile. On 12 March he wrote the following characteristic letter to his 'Dear Dad':

I received your topping letter last night, for which I thank you. Well, now we are all whonkey just now, and I am finding it very cold sitting in my shop billet. To-day I can find heaps of time for writing, for we are just walking about waiting for the snow to stop. We have now waited two days, and look like waiting another two. All the Transport left, so we have not even got any kit. All I have is a big cake and a bottle of brilliantine. Not much joy, is it? However, we have got round the old cook at our billet, and she will see that we get plenty to eat, but it is beastly having nothing to do, not even a book to read.

We shall get off first chance we get. I had a rum go yesterday. I was sent on a patrol, although the clouds were so low and full of snow. I arrived over the lines, and in about two seconds was lost in a thick cloud. I was in this cloud for nearly half an hour, not knowing what I was doing. 'However, I came out in the end, and on looking down, saw I was well over the Hun lines at 500 feet. This was rotten, or at least my observer thought so, for he was so upset that he was quite unable to work the gun. I was about five minutes finding my bearings, and during this time, the old Huns gave us the very devil of a time, the whole Hun lines being ablaze with rifle fire. We could actually see their faces and see them rush up the trench when I put my nose down, for they thought they had hit us and stopped firing at once. That was the thing I wanted, for I put my nose up again at once, and got into the cloud and over our lines again.

The Major nearly had a fit and asked me what I was doing over the lines at that height, for we are not allowed over there under 7,000 feet. He also asked me what good we did by going over, so I said 'Oh! no good, we only caused every German in the trench to feel sick, also to use about a hundred pounds of shot.' He had to laugh, but naturally, it was a mad thing to do, and we should not have done it if the cloud had not been there, but it was sport.

Next time I shall have an observer who will work the gun, for I have now found a good man, who wishes to fly with me as an observer.

Well, I cannot tell you of any very exciting experiences, for I have not had any in the last few days, but I hope for a good smack soon.

I ought to tell you that our machine was not hit once. Really, I could hardly believe my eyes on landing. I expected it to be covered.

Thank you so much for sending me things each week. You are a topper, and not only me but the Mess think so; in fact, we think each other's people are toppers, for they send us such ripping things.

Now, re dear old Cyril; he is just the kind of chap we want out here, heaps of go. You just tell him that he is not to think about me so much, for you can bet I shall be alright and look after myself.

Well, Dad, I must close now, for not only have I used all my paper; but I am very cold.

The postscript to this letter relates to a subject to which he often referred: 'P.S. – Your remark in your letter about God looking after me is quite right, for I think it is God and not only luck.'

An airman's life about this time – if it was enviable compared to that of the man in the trenches – was hardly comfortable:

March 13th, 1916.

Dearest Lol,

We are stuck at this place and cannot get to our new Flying ground on account of the snow, and, really, I have never been so cold in all my life. No fire, and not even hot lunch. To-night I shall try walking to a certain place, about 10 k.'s away, and if I get there I will try and get you some little thing (cannot tell you the name of the place for we are not allowed).

Re speaking French, naturally I can speak like a native now? You would love to see this place, about every house is a ruin, and even the church is smashed up. Most interesting, but not nice when they try a few bombs on the place.

It is very good of you to send the books, and the Mess love you for doing so.

I am very sorry to hear you have had the Zepps. again, but, really, I cannot stop them, so you will have to put up with it.

Well, bon jour, dear, I must dry up now.

Ever your loving Brother.

On 20 March his machine was brought down by enemy gunfire, but although both he and the observer were imprisoned in the wreckage, they escaped unhurt. He was more interested in a bath he had had in a hay-loft:

March 21st & 22nd, 1916.

My dearest Sister,

Have just had a bath in my hay-loft. I say hay-loft, for I am now billetted in one. However, I am making it quite nice, for I really think that we shall be at this place for a long time.

We have now been here for about four days. The first night I slept in a house, but it was such a dirty place that I have now taken a hay-loft.

I am not going to tell you about the working side of our life out there, for you can read about that from father's letters. I received another parcel to-day, and we have made very quick work with it.

Re photo, I am giving it to you, but I think a great deal about it, for a great many of my pals, alive and otherwise, are on it. It was taken on March 17th at our last flying ground. The machine in the background is mine, but yesterday it was hit, and is now a total wreck, but my observer was not hurt and you bet I was not. However, it was a very near thing, for we were trapped in the wreckage.

I got a lot of pieces of shell in my machine in my last patrol. They do not look very big, but just imagine thousands of them flying around you, also the explosion that takes place in order to break the shell into such small pieces. On this trip we both got off without a scratch, but the machine did not.

Re the tablier enclosed, after the crash yesterday I had half a day off, so took the chance and walked to the nearest village, five miles away, in order to get it. I think it will look sweet if worn with a white dress. All the girls have them on for afternoon tea out here, but naturally they are not made of silk, but they look topping. I think that I must close, for the chaps are calling me to join them.

There were great possibilities about that hay-loft, and Ball set about furnishing it.

March 30th, 6.30 p.m., 1916.

My dear Lol,

Have just received your top-hole letter. As you say, hay-lofts can be made quite nice. I have made mine ripping now, but things cost such a lot out here, everyone is on the make. I have fixed curtains up, with big pink bows, also I have covered everything with blue cloth. I bought a stove a few days ago, and although I cannot see for smoke at times it is quite nice.

Please look in a drawer in my bedroom and you will find a brown paper parcel full of photos. Will you please send it out to me, for I want to put them round my hut.

Yes, my girl, your old gee-gee will kill you yet. Why will you not be good? I bet you put a pin in it in order to make it run away, but I suppose you will get over it.

I was hit with a very large piece of shell a few days ago. It smashed one of my cylinders and stopped my engine.

Be good, heaps of love.

Those curtains, bows, and photographs, were wanted to make his place seem more like the home he loved!

Building his hut in France.

CHAPTER 6

The 'Crisis' of the Fokker

Ball hints at the menace of the Fokker machines in these days, although apparently they fought shy of him even at this early stage. In a letter quoted later in this volume he says, 'Our machines stand no chance with a Fokker.'

In another letter to his sister in February he said, 'Re my machine, I like it a bit better now, but it is not fast enough. You see the Hun Fokker can go twice as fast, so we get second in most of the fights and the Hun comes out first. However, my usual luck will come along with me I hope.'

The Fokker sensation began just about the close of 1915. It was short lived, but for a few weeks the German machine had a great advertisement. It was the invention of a Dutchman, who offered an early design to the British Government, who rejected it because it was such an inferior machine that it would have been unfair to have asked a British pilot to trust his life with it. The Dutchman accordingly went to Germany, and eventually produced an entirely new model – a copy of the French Morane monoplane fitted with very powerful engines. It was no longer inherently stable, and consequently could turn much more quickly. Perhaps the best account of its powers and limitations was contained in an official report issued by the Flying Corps in France in January, when the attention of the public was being attracted. It stated:

The Fokker is a monoplane especially built and contrived for fighting and for pursuit of the enemy, to which duties its activities are by strict order confined and for which it is specially adapted on account of its high speed. It is not allowed to expose itself by venturing over our lines on reconnaissance work.

But there were ominous signs in the official communiques that the air campaign was not going well, notably on 14 January, when the communique stated, 'Four of our aeroplanes sent out yesterday have not returned.'

A German official report, issued on 29 January, gave these figures of the air casualties since 1 October:

	Allied	German
Shot down	11	8
Lost in air fights	41	7
Missing	—	1
Captured	11	—
	63	16

It was doubtful whether these figures were accurate – the German losses were probably much heavier – but they nevertheless indicated that the war in the air was far from satisfactory for the Allies. Compare these figures with the British official in February 1918, when 138 German machines were 'accounted for' and only thirty-nine British machines were 'missing,' and it will be seen how the conditions have changed since Ball first fought.

During the early stages of the Verdun struggle the German machines undoubtedly met with considerable success. The two outstanding Fokker artists were Immelmann and Boelcke. They were the air idols of Germany, and claimed many victims.

In England it was declared that our flying men, the best in the world, were being out-engined and out-powered 'by the deadly Fokkers'. There was a demand that more encouragement should be given the manufacturers to turn out faster machines, 'in preference to the official obsolete types.' Ball himself was pessimistic about the situation. Writing on 22 March he said:

> They say things are very bad in France just now, and I am afraid we shall all get a hotting up this time. The Hun R.F.C. is far ahead of us, in fact about 30 m.p.h. Oh, I do wish I had got my own machine. I am getting a machine here ready. I am taking one gun off in order to take off weight, and also I am lowering the wind screen in order to take off head resistance. A great many things I am taking off in the hope that I shall get a little better control and speed.

It was not long before the inferiority had been largely remedied. At the Air Enquiry held in July, General Henderson stated: 'Since February or March we have had a large number of machines superior to the Fokker.'

He was asked: 'Why were more British machines than German brought down at one time?'

The General replied: 'Because we were doing the work of the Army, and the Germans were not. They were trying to stop us.'

In January, Mr Tennant, who was then Under Secretary for War, had said that the defensive nature of German methods of fighting in the air must be kept in mind. 'If the Germans attempt an offensive,' he said, 'and come behind our lines, we have a machine quite equal in efficiency and speed to the Fokker aeroplane, which they employ defensively behind the lines.'

He stated that in four weeks we used 138 machines as compared with the enemy's twenty, and that whereas 1,227 of our machines crossed the German lines, only 310 Germans crossed ours.

Before the summer the Fokker's reputation had suffered a serious set-back, and very much less was heard of the exploits of Immelmann and Boelcke. Immelmann was killed in June in a fight with a British airman, and Boelcke perished in the following October in a collision in mid-air.

The British communique of 28 June showed how things had changed:

Yesterday in the air numerous hostile aircraft were encountered on the enemy's side of the line. Five of our machines engaged four Fokkers, two of which were brought down and fell out of control. Four more of the enemy's machines were driven down in the course of the day. Our casualties – one machine missing.

A great achievement in March was the bringing down of three Fokkers by Lieut. Eustace Grenfell.

The best explanation of the whole question of supremacy in the air was furnished by Major Baird in the House of Commons on 26 April 1917:

The mastery of the air is a phrase having very little meaning. There is really no such thing, for not only is the air a very big space, but for the purpose of aircraft it is becoming bigger every day. No-one will pretend that it is practicable to patrol a strip of air a hundred miles long and five miles deep in such a way as to make it impossible for the enemy to get below or above the patrol ... What can be done is to ensure that our airmen shall enjoy a degree of predominance sufficient to enable them to carry out their duties and to prevent the Germans carrying out their duties.

Ball with all his recognition of the formidable qualities of the Fokker was nevertheless anxious to get at close quarters, although he had had as yet no experience of single-handed fighting. The following letters describe some more of his early adventures, when he says he always sang when up above the clouds.

Now I will tell you a bit about our most topping life here. First of all the bright side, for we always look on the bright side.

We arrived here on Sunday, but expect to get away in a few days.

Now, our next flit will be the last, for we go to our new flying ground next time. We are only just behind the lines, so we do not have far to fly in order to get on to our working front, but the guns are going all day and night, and make a rotten row.

The day we arrived a lot of Hun machines came over the lines, dropping bombs all the way. Four of them dropped just behind our billet, but did no damage.

The day before yesterday I had quite a good time. We were on a patrol over the Hun lines at 9,000 feet, when a Hun Fokker machine passed right under my machine. I rushed after him, but he would not fight, but rushed over his own lines at once, so we could not have a smack.

Yesterday we had a long patrol over the Hun lines. We had a rotten time, every machine was hit, and only five out of six returned.

(I must dry up for a few seconds. One of the observers in our Flight have just brought the post in. Yes, I thought so, how ripping of you. I have just received a tophole parcel of things, so you bet I am now A1, for we do so like receiving letters).

Now to continue my letter. I will just tell you exactly what took place on the patrol.

We started at 10 a.m., got our height, and started out over the lines.

There were six machines on the job, one doing the observing, and the other five defending.

We started with bad luck, for as soon as we got over the lines we were shot at by Archie guns, and every machine was hit, but not enough to prevent us from going on. However, their next move put things poo-poo, for they sent a lot of Hun machines up to fight us. Two Fokkers were with them, and as our machines stand no chance with a Fokker, we knew at once that one of us would be done for. Naturally, we all put up a good scrap, but one of our machines was about a quarter of a mile behind. One of the Fokkers attacked it, and we just heard tap-tap-tap for a few seconds. At this point we made the other Huns run away, and we turned round to help the rear machine. However, all too late, for the observer was killed, and the machine crashed on landing. The pilot was a brick, for although he had been in for such a rotten time, he managed to get over our lines before crashing.

The Fokker ran away when we turned, or the pilot would also have been done for.

The remaining five machines got back, but we were all hit in quite a lot of places. I was hit by six shots and one piece of shell, but with my usual luck did not get any great damage.

Well, now I will not go on telling you about our beastly luck,' for, really, we do not like talking about it. Quite a lot of machines have been brought down in the last few days.

Well, now for more joyous news.

Last night I was just getting into my bed when a sponge full of water came along the room. At once the place was in a fine mess. I threw a jug of water, but the same was returned with interest. Next the place got so full of water that I ran into the garden, falling into a big hole full of mud. I managed to obtain two onions on my way back, and with these attacked the mob. All our beds were wet through. However, at last all got right again and we got our sleep. *It was great sport.*

In this billet we sleep and live seven in a small room, sleeping on the floor. Well, now is all very well, and you have no need to bother about me, but do please send me heaps of letters, and please do not think me mean if I do not send a lot in return, for after our work we really do want a rest, and do not wish to think about anything. But on the Q.T., I tell you, never am I more happy than when I am writing to my dear people.

This last letter reflects the undaunted spirit of the boys who were fighting against heavy odds in these days. 'Beastly luck' was apparently the hardest thing Ball had to say about the conditions in which they had to fight.

When almost every day pilots went out never to return, and the Fokker was making the most of the fleeting advantage it possessed, these boys so far from being depressed were playing dormitory larks and indulging in wild 'rags.'

The discomforts of their billets were merely subjects for humour.

Ball went into more details about the bad smash he had on 20 March, mentioned in the previous chapter, and describes the fate that befell a comrade who was not so fortunate:

March 21st & 22nd.

At last I have had a near thing. On March 20th my dear old machine was done in. We both had a very near escape, for we were trapped in the wreckage.

For the last day and night I have been up at the trenches with my machine packed away in the corner of a wood, so that the Huns would not see it. Only a few feet from the wood a machine landed yesterday, but he was not lucky enough to get his machine under cover, and the Huns got him on the 25th, shot, and set the machine on fire.

I started back at 4 o'clock this morning, and was flying about 6 a.m. I could only go up 500 feet on account of the clouds, but with my usual luck, I did not crash, but I was very pleased to get back.

To-day we can do no flying, for the clouds are only about 50 feet up, so we expect to get some little time for writing letters. I received another parcel yesterday, for which I thank you very much. I really cannot write more, although I have heaps to say. I always try to get to sleep at 10, and I will not break down now. Be good. Good-night.

The greatest moment in the life of a young airman is when he can lay claim to having 'got a Hun.' Then he becomes a veritable knight of the air, worthy of his wings. Ball had yet to claim his first victim.

Towards the end of March he was hoping to bring down his first enemy machine, but he pointed out that the machine he was flying was not for fighting. He was still patrolling and spotting for the artillery, but nevertheless on the look-out for a fight even in the slow machine he was piloting:

March 26th.

How are you to-day? Really, I am so sorry to be taking so long in sending you another letter, but it cannot be helped. I have only just been told that it is Sunday; we cannot tell one day from another out here. Oh, I would just love to go to church to-day; however, that will come later.

Do please look after yourselves, for I would sooner have you than all the cash in all the world. So please give up a few of your jobs. You say that I do not know how you would like to see my old face again. Oh, yes I do, and in time you will see it. I shall get leave in about eight weeks' time. Really, I think that I shall go mad when I am on the way home. We are supposed to get seven days every three months, but we are lucky if we get it every year, so I shall be very satisfied if I get leave in two or three months' time.

You say that you wish that I could bring down a Hun machine. So do I, but our machines are not for fighting, and it is the Hun who comes out top. However, I have got a good observer with heaps of pluck, so we shall get a chance one day before long. Last night we went over the lines together looking for a scrap, but we saw nothing to attack.

The Squadron is now on patrol and battery work. We do a shoot in the day, and at night go round the battery and see how things went. I went round last night, and found it most interesting. You see we now get trench work as well as our flying.

The eggs you sent me were top hole. We all had one for tea to-day.

Apparently, Ball was quite unable to appreciate the anxiety that his letters caused his parents. To him at this time the danger of the air was not very far removed from that of a kick in the football field; it never troubled him. He sent accounts of his narrow escapes to interest and amuse his parents. When these drew from Mr Ball, senior, reply full of anxiety as to his son's danger, Ball wrote threatening to send only uninteresting letters.

My dear Dad [he wrote on March 29th],

Now you are in for a blowing up, for I am very cross with you. I can see from your letter, which has just arrived, that you trouble yourself about me, and think that I am not safe. Well, now, please understand that if you bother or trouble yourself any more, I will not tell you any more things that take place. I shall just send short un-interesting letters, just like I used to.

So you think to come down in my machine was a bit too real to be pleasant. So it was, but this morning I had a much better time. My observer and I started out in artillery work. After being over the lines for about half an hour, at a height of 8,000 feet, I saw a Hun at 5,000 feet. My observer got the guns on him, and I dived down at him. However, from above we heard another gun going, and on looking up we saw another Hun coming down from above. It was one of their tricks. They wanted me to fight the lower machine, and the one above would come up behind and do me in. We got 100 shots into the lower machine, and it dived down to earth, but did not crash. The machine above let fly at us, but only smashed an engine bearer wire; it then ran off for we got the other gun going. We had another look round this afternoon, but saw nothing. Please tell Cyril that perhaps he had better stick to his regiment. I like this job, but nerves do not last long, and you soon want a rest.

Re souvenirs. So you want one, do you? I will let you have the first bit that comes to stay, but so many that hit go straight through. However, I will go over and get a bit for you.

The trick he mentions was tried many times afterwards by the Germans, in effort to trap Ball. Many enemy machines have come to grief in this manoeuvre. On this occasion he nearly got his first victim.

It is curious to note that Ball was evidently rather doubtful whether his nerves would stand the strain, but it was about the only occasion he expressed such a fear.

He was flying in a two-seater machine at this time, and General Higgins has explained in his appreciation at the beginning of this volume that Ball was essentially a single-handed fighter, and much preferred fighting by himself to being one of a patrol.

However apprehensive he may have been there is no sign of an impending breakdown in the letters that follow. April begun with much bustle in the air, and Ball was very busy.

'Going over' to face the enemy fire in order to get a souvenir in the shape of a piece of shrapnel in his machine, was the sort of errand that was to Ball the most natural thing in the world.

Since these letters were written the country has learnt a great deal about the life of our airmen, but in 1916 the public knew very little of their daily work. It is nothing now for a pilot to leave France in the morning, have lunch in London, and get back to his mess dinner in France the same evening, after having made various reports to people on both sides of the Channel.

Even so this glimpse of Ball leaving a letter unfinished until his return from a two hours' patrol over the enemy lines with shrapnel bursting all about his machine and a Fokker perhaps hovering above expecting to get another victim, is a bit startling.

April 1st, 11 a.m.

Oh! life is a rush out here. Well, I have a lot to tell you, but I have another patrol now, so I must finish this letter to-night. Since my last letter to Dad, I have had three more fights, also a trip round the Batteries with the Major. All took place yesterday. This makes four fights in one week.

(Continued April 2nd, Sunday).

Hello, Mother,

I have just come in from a rat shoot. We have great sport shooting rats out here. Nearly every night we take torch and revolver, and always manage to kill a few. I have only done one patrol to-day, in fact, I have had a very slack day. It has been very hot, so hot that we only just managed to walk from the billet to our machines.

Well, now I wanted to send you a long letter, but dinner is on the table, so I must depart.

April 3rd, 4.15 p.m.

To-day I have been having a slack, for we cannot fly on account of the rain, etc. It is the first bad day for a long time, so we are all having a good rest. Part of the morning I spent in spring cleaning my hut. It would make you laugh if you could see me, for I have everything spotlessly clean, even if I have to stay up all night to get it so. I have got a nice gramaphone, and this afternoon a few of the chaps have been in, so we played the gramaphone and finished a huge box of chocolates which came to-day. Thanks so much, they were topping. I am all A1 now.

I shall be getting my leave in about four weeks, so please get all O.K. by then.

'We often do strange things out here, in fact, we are a strange people,' wrote Ball one afternoon after having what he calls, 'A mud and brick end fight with a pal.' This was a few minutes before he had his first victories in air fights. He does not enthuse over them, because in each case the enemy was able to land and were not destroyed. All the same, it was as he described it, 'A topping time.'

'We did our patrol,' he said, 'and afterwards went round a big factory about five miles behind the lines.'

A letter to his sister relates the bringing down of two Hun machines, but he is very careful not to make any claim that the

Germans were destroyed. He had seen the sun set from his seat in the clouds, and had waited until it was dark before coming down.

April 9th, 1916.

My dear Lol,

I have had quite an exciting time to-day. One of our games was to attack a Hun balloon. We put a drum of five shots into it.

Last night I was on a patrol from 5 until 7.30 p.m. It was most interesting to see the sun set. When I came down it was quite dark.

Well, dear, you must excuse short letter, for I really cannot get time for more.

It was great sport, and most interesting. After that I went for the post, and to my great joy found two parcels from you. They were topping, and we had a ripping tuck in.

Things are much better in the Mess now, but parcels are very welcome. After the tuck in I had a bath in my barn, and now I am writing letters.

It has been very hot the last few days, but to-day is very cold.

Three machines belonging to our ground have been brought down, and the pilots done in. Our Squadron is very lucky, we have not lost any just lately. A great many Huns have been close in. Yesterday one was brought down, pilot and observer killed. I managed to beg the prism out of the pilot's field glasses. In the Combat Report for the last two weeks, it states that two Huns were made to land by a B.E. 2. Names of pilot and observer are not mentioned, but it is Lieutenant G. and me, and Lieutenant V. and me. Names are only mentioned when the machines are seen to crash, and we did not see it crash, for I think they got down all right. Well, I must close for to-night, but will continue tomorrow.

April 6th, 10.30 p.m.

Hello, Dad,

We are not flying just now on account of the clouds being only 1,000 feet up. However, it is a good chance to write letters. I am just doing the vanishing trick with the box of figs you sent yesterday. If we are not flying this afternoon, three of us are going to a certain big town just behind the lines. It will be most interesting for it is shelled every day, and nearly every house has been hit. We are going to try and find a house with a bath in it. If we do we shall get the steam up and have a bath. In heaps of the houses you find rooms all in order, so you bet we shall have a topping time. Before long we are moving into huts, so I shall have to give up my clean old barn.

Please let me know how the works are going on. I can see things being pretty rotten after this war if one is not on the look out. Well, so much for money matters, I must not get too serious.

All is going fine now, and with luck I shall be home within two months for a ten days' leave. Oh! will it not be topping?

Ball even found time to do business out there; he was always ready to do a deal of some kind however pressing other claims on his time might be.

In one communication he writes, 'A few lines on most important subjects. Have you any more Beeston land? - any small bit of good building land will do; it must be near a town or a village, also cheap. This is for one of our pilots, but I think that if you send me a few particulars, I can sell quite a lot to our officers.' In the same letter he talks of a new machine. The machine was subsequently accepted by the Government.

I have the plans now of a most wonderful machine. It will be heaps better than the Hun Fokker. I have been to the Major, and he has given me full permission to fly it if I get one out. I know that it will be a fine thing. Well, things are topping just now, but clouds, etc., are putting a big stop to our game.

I managed to put a 20lb. bomb in a C. trench the day before yesterday, but otherwise I have had no real job, but it will get fine before long, I hope.

I have just had my hair cut by the Squadron barber. It was topping, for he pulls it out in handfulls. However, it was quite nice.

Well, I have been nearly driven whonkey in the last few days, for letters have been so very short, but to-day I was full up with joy. Oh! you do not know how topping it is to get letters from our dear ones. Well, dear, your letter made me so pleased, and you bet I read them so many times I nearly wore the writing off. Well, I have very little news, for we have not done much flying in the last few days. I managed to pop a 20lb. bomb into a G. trench a few days ago, and that is all of late. However, luck is topping, and God is good, so all is fine.

That optimistic 'however' was invariably evident.

Rat-hunting, the prospect of flying a new fast machine, a fight with a Hun Albatross, some exciting Hun-hunts, are described in the extracts that follow here:

April 17th.

I have just been out rat-hunting. It was great sport, but I only got one rat. I found a big French gun when first I came here, and this is the article I use for the job. You say that you would like to see me in my barn having a bath. Well, I am just about to have another, so you may come. My barn is very nice now, but I think we are going into huts in a few days, so all barns will be given up.

Re a Hun keepsake; yes, I will get one. I have got a few but not very good ones. I have got the prism out of a Hun's field-glasses. He was brought down a few days ago, and both pilot and observer were killed.

We are the wireless squadron now, and have to register the gun shots. It is a most important job, but we do not get many chances to tackle the Huns. However, luck may come. For one thing, my machine is not a fighting machine.

Lieutenant V— has just come into my barn, so he now expects me to finish my letter and talk to him, but I tell him letter first, so he is sitting on my bed looking at a mag. Well, I have very little to say for things are slack just now. Will write again in a few days. Well, must close now, or V— will go mad.

Towards the end of April he began to see better days ahead. His wish to fly a single-seater was soon to be granted, and then for 'the great sport.' Meanwhile, there was not much fighting, and Ball was employed on experimental work, trying new devices.

April 23rd.

Well, how are things? I am now shut up in the orderly room, for I am O.P. It is a rotten job, for we never have any work to do. No Zepp. ever comes over here.

I am not having a bad time, and I can see better days in the near future. You know that I do not like the B.E. machines. Well, each day I have asked the Major to let me fly the Scout. He always said no, but to-day I hear that I am going to a certain aerodrome to fly a new Morane Scout bullet. If all is well, I shall be back at No. 13 in about a month's time, and my mount will be a Morane, which will do 120 m.p.h. This will be great sport, and at last I shall have the chance I wish for. I do not know what day I go yet, it may be in two or three weeks, or perhaps a day, but go I shall in the end.

Things have been very slack of late. I had a bit of a scrap yesterday, but nothing any good. At present I have got the experimental machine of the squadron. It is very interesting to try the new things that come out nearly every day, but I cannot say that it is exactly nice, for they fit such mad things on.

Well, old sport, news is scarce just now, so I will dry up. Will write again soon.

For the first time apparently, Ball engaged in a fight at such close quarters that he could see the faces of his opponents. The opposing machines were only a few feet apart, and the struggle was short and sharp. Later on in some of his fights, he got so close to his enemies that collisions seemed certain. It was then that he showed his great nerve. When they saw his machine dashing straight for them, seemingly quite indifferent whether there was a smash-up in mid-air, most of the Huns turned and bolted.

He tells of the irresistible impulse to sing when above the clouds. It must have been the same feeling of exaltation which made a comrade write:

In joy that on these flashing wings
I cleave the skies – O! let them fret –
Now know I why the skylark sings
Untrammelled in the boundless air –
For mine it is his bliss to share.[1]

Ball learnt to fly in order to kill, but that was only an accident. His joy in flying was innocent of the lust to kill.

April 28th & May 3rd.

I only returned from 1st A.D. last night, and to-day I have commenced well by bringing a Hun down. I was doing a patrol at the time in a B.E. 2.c. Five Huns came at first, but we made them run; later a Hun two-seater Albatross came. I rushed my machine at it, and got within a few feet. He fired, we fired … However, he only got time for five shots, for the observer was then killed.

The interesting point about it was that we could see the Huns' faces, and they could see ours, we were so near.

After the observer was killed, the pilot rushed down, but I think he was not hurt very badly. Lieutenant V— was my observer, so you bet he is pleased with life.

Well, now I fly the fighting Bristol Scout, so I shall get a few better chances. I have no passenger, you see.

At times I shall fly also my B.E. 2.c., but only for wireless jobs.

Excuse more as I have only a few seconds on hand.

P.S. – Tell Cyril it is great sport, but home is better.

Things are now going fine, and I have at last got a morning off, for it is raining.

Since 9 a.m. I have been spring cleaning my hut. You would be very surprised to see how topping it looks. I have put all the photographs up from home. I have also got a gramaphone.

So you sang all the way from Woodhall when you were driving the little car. That is topping, and you must have been happy. I always sing when up above the clouds, it is very nice. But I am always happy, so it is not strange. But I am just beginning to want a few days at home. Oh! I shall be pleased to see you all, really I shall nearly go mad with joy.

Everything is going fine, and I think you such a dear old sport to work so hard for me.

It is very whonkey about one of our men being killed, but as you say one must put up with a few troubles.

Re the works, I think we had better keep the copper, for this war will not end yet. Please do not sell it.

Re aeroplane, plans will be sent on in a few days.

On 3 May he wrote home to tell his sister that he had killed a Hun, and that the Germans were poor fighters in the air.

I am going on O.K., and hope to be home for a few days in about four weeks' time. Will it not be fine? I do so want to see your dear faces again.

I managed to kill a Hun a few days ago. It was a good fight, but the Huns are rather N.G. as regards fighting in the air. I have got most of the day off on account of rain, so I am trying to get in tons of writing. We are now in huts, my hut is very nice.

You know that I have just finished at the 1st A.D. flying the fighting scout. I had only had two fights with my squadron when one of our chaps went up in it and crashed it. I am now on a B.E. 2.c. again until a new one comes.

What it means to a pilot to fly a defective machine over the German lines is an experience which Ball and his comrades knew to their cost.

The noise that was made about the Fokker was accompanied by considerable criticism about the faulty construction of some of the British machines. Ball does not conceal his troubles, though he blamed nobody. His luck and skill carried him safely through.

Also being such a keen mechanic himself and constantly working on his own machines when he was not flying, he prevented many accidents that might have proved fatal to himself. He never took foolish risks with a machine, and when he flew the confidence he had in it was born of intimate knowledge of the engine and the various parts of the aeroplane. In the following letter he describes a nasty accident which he could scarcely have foreseen, as it was due to the inaccurate timing of the gun on his new machine fixed to fire through the propeller. It was only by a fluke that he did not have to land in the enemy lines:

May 6th.

You ask me to send you a long letter, even if I stay up all night in order to do it.

Well, after my work was finished last night, I did stay up and I did write a long letter for you, but this morning I burnt it, for I am not pleased with it.

I went up in my new Scout yesterday, and over the lines I fired my gun. The fool thing had not been timed right, and all the shots went through the propeller. When I arrived back, my propeller was nearly in two. This means that if I had fired about six more shots I should have had to land in Hun land, for I could never have got back. After this I went up in my B.E. 2.c. I had just got up when the engine went wrong; I only just got back on the aerodrome.

Re plans for new machine, we cannot send plans by post, so I shall bring them when I come home on leave. The Major thinks it a topping brain-wave.

Well, old chap, I will not bore you any longer.

His misfortunes were not at an end, and they must have been particularly galling seeing that they were concerned with the new single-seater fighting machines that he had been longing for.

He had scarcely begun to take his toll of the German airmen, but he was already chasing them away repeatedly. The trouble he was having with his machines was getting on his nerves much more than the strain of constant fighting subsequently did. He tells of one disappointment when two enemy machines actually ventured close to the aerodrome and he was sent up after them:

May, 1916.

Well, now I have tons to say, but am very tired, for I was at work at 3.30 this morning. However, I am now sitting under a hedge resting, at the same time writing. So do excuse pencil. I will commence from yesterday afternoon. General H— came over, he sent for me and congratulated me on my work, also for bringing the Hun down. He also said that a machine called a Bullet was coming in a few days, and I am to fly it. This will make the third fighting Scout I have been given to fly. I have not brought any other machine down on my latest machine yet, but I have chased a lot; however, they ran away.

Now, for to-day's news. I was told to be on the 4.15 patrol, so I got up at 3.30. On getting out I saw our A.A. guns firing at two Huns nearly over our aerodrome. Naturally, I got very excited, for they do not often come over now. My Nieuport was got ready and I went up. Got up 10,000 ft. in 10 mins., and got ready to chase. My gun cable smashed, and I had to return. My Bristol was next got out and I went up again, but this machine is much slower. However, I got up to them and chased them over their lines, but was unable to get near enough to fire. On turning to come back I found that I could not see the ground, also I was about forty miles from the aerodrome. I got back in about two hours.

The Major met me and told me to get off to bed, for I am to fly again from 5–7. Oh! we have got a topping major. Well, I have not gone to bed, but am resting and writing.

Re leave, I must say that although my nerves are quite good, I really do want a rest from all this work. I can stand a lot, but, really, I have been coming on in leaps and bounds in the last few days, and it is just beginning to tell on me. I always feel tired.

Well, now enough about myself. I have just received a topping parcel, thanks so much. You can think of me taking a pocket full of cake every morning on my patrol, for I always eat cake when excited.

I have struck a topping lot of chaps in this squadron, and they look after me fine, but they all think me young and call me John. Well, this is no hardship, and I am very happy.

Now, I think I will close and have an hour's sleep, so that I shall be in working order to-night.

Do please give my love to my dear mother, and tell her that I am coming home soon.

P.S. – Garden going topping, and such a real pleasure.

The expected leave did not come off; instead he was given yet another new machine, a French product, which sent him into ecstacies and led him to exclaim, 'Huns, look out!'

May 7th.

Am having a long day of it to-day. I was over the Hun lines at 3.45 a.m. on patrol.

Well, I have only got a few seconds in which to write this letter, so I will get on with my real subject. At last my luck has gone a bit whonkey. I have received orders to go to No. 11 and fly a new French machine, so this means the end of my leave. Oh! I am poo-poo, for I do so want a rest. However, it may be a great chance, so I will put a grin on and do what bit I can.

The machine is one of the fastest going. Will write again later. Shall get leave in about another three or four months.

2.30 p.m.

Hello, I have just had lunch - lunched out, for I was asked into another flight's mess. Now, to finish my letter. It is still raining, but I have got a machine to test at 4 o'clock.

Yesterday, at 5 a.m., one of our machines came down. Observer was killed at once, pilot was badly smashed about.

5.30 p.m.

Oh! I am quite whonkey now. Have just been up to test my new machine. The new engine and under-carriage are now on. Well, I have never had such sport. I fooled about and banked it, having such a topping test ride. It is T.T. So Huns, *look out!*

Must dry up now, for I am very excited, and only want a fine dry day.

The first time he destroyed a Hun machine is recorded on 15 May, when he destroyed an Albatross.

You will be pleased to hear [he said] that I brought down a Hun Albatross. He was at 5,000 feet over his lines, I was at 12,000. I dived down at him and put 120 shots into the machine, after which he turned over and was completely done in.

After the fight I was only 3,000 feet up, and my engine was missing, but with my usual luck I got back. There is another new machine out now, a French make. I am going to fly it soon, for it is much faster than mine. I think I have talked enough shop, so will now answer your letter. Since I started writing this, two of our pilots have just crashed, but they are not hurt, so all is well.

His new machine, he said, was one of the best England or France could give a pilot: 'I flew it for the first time yesterday afternoon, and did very well. When it lands it hits the ground at 80 m.p.h., so you can guess what speed it goes in the air. It is a single-seater with 110 h.p. engine, so I have no observer to keep safe.'

Hereabouts our casualties were heavy, the Fokker was still giving a lot of trouble, but the day of vengeance was drawing near.

A letter to his sister and brother on 16 May tells a tragic story of heavy losses. He asks them not to let their parents see it, realising that it would add very much to their anxiety about himself:

May 16th, 1916.

My Dearest Lol and Cill,

Do please excuse me not writing two letters, but really things are desperate just now, and my mind is full up with poo-poo thoughts. I have just lost such a dear old pal, Capt. Lucas. He was brought down by a Fokker last night about 5 p.m. Now, don't show Mother or Dad this letter, and I will then tell you about the fights.

The Fokker came up behind the B.E. from the rear. It opened fire, and at once hit Capt. Lucas, who was the observer. Lieut. Wright was pilot, and such a fine chap. He kept at his job, although he was hit in the shoulder. Fifty shots the Fokker fired, but Lieut. Wright got over our side and landed, walked out a few yards and then fell down. Capt. Lucas died in a few hours. The machine was brought back this morning, and I am not exaggerating when I say that it was soaked in blood, and full of bullet holes.

No. 11, my squadron, lost six machines yesterday and one crashed to-day. Only one out of our flight is missing, and he was such a topping chap.

Now, for a bit of cheerful news. I was on patrol yesterday morning on my British Scout. I was at 12,000 ft. and saw a Hun at 5,000. It started off and I went after it, catching it up when twenty miles over its own lines. It took 120 shots to do it in, but in the end it went down, upside down. I got back, but was Archied badly. In the afternoon I received orders to fly a new French machine. Did well on it, so they are now getting one for me. This means that I shall be on one of the best machines England and France can give a pilot, so I hope for a good run.

Good-bye, you dears.

A few days later he had good news for his 'Mother and Dad':

> May 24th.
>
> I was just getting out of my machine last night when a warrant was brought for me, saying that I could go on leave to-day. Naturally, I nearly went mad with joy, but I saw the Major this morning, and he said that he was so sorry, but my leave must be put off again, for I was wanted.
>
> This put the stopper on all things for a few seconds, but after a second's thinking, I decided that it was only right that I should not go. It is hard luck, but this comes about because I fly the Nieuport, and we have only two pilots who do fly it. Now, the Major will do his best, so you can expect a wire any day saying that I am in England.
>
> Now, Dad, when you hear that A. Ball, junior, is on his way home, just you pack your traps at once and away we go in order to get our health back. Any old place will do, so long as we get tons of fishing. I get a week in England, and two can do a lot in a week.
>
> I do hope Mother will also give up all and come for a rest.

It is a most surprising fact, but when one's leave is drawing near, we are always very afraid of being done in, for it would be bad luck to just miss leave, and get a bullet.

However, you will see my old clock in a few days, so all is well. I shall have tons of tales to tell.

Then he wrote lamenting the disappearance of old comrades, and went on to say:

My dear old pal came back yesterday. Oh! I am so pleased, for we are nearly brothers. He brought me a huge box of chocolates, also a new cap.

My old squadron, No. 13, and my new one, No. 11, are on the same aerodrome, so we can often see each other.

Well, now I will tell you just a little of No. 13 and No. n luck of yesterday and to-day. Yesterday, we lost six machines, and No. 13 lost one. One of my dear friends was brought down in No. 13. Fifty shots were put into his machine by a Fokker. Pilot was only wounded, but passenger was killed.

It is a strange thing, but in one week every chap in B Flight of No. 13 Squadron has been replaced by a new man from England. When Lieut. V— came back he knew no one.

In our squadron, No. 11, my Flight Commander only lost one man. He crashed a machine in the morning, and this made him so cross that he went up at 5 o'clock in the afternoon and swore that he would bring down a Hun. He has not been seen since. Poor chap, he was such a topper.

So far, only one of our machines has been done in to-day. This makes seven in two days. Well, don't get wind up for I am all right, and if I do well I shall be home in a few days now.

Yesterday I brought an Albatross Hun down, twenty miles over Hun land, with my Bristol, so you bet my latest machine will do well.

Shall be home soon.

He did not get leave until three weeks later, and a few weeks before the Western front burst into flame with the first great battle of the Somme.

Notes

1. From 'The Joy of Flying', Paul Bewsher, RNAS.

Next page: Captain Ball with the propeller of an aeroplane in which he brought down his first fourteen enemy machines and the large red steel nose-cap used for distinguishing purposes.

CHAPTER 7

Everywhere in France

Albert Ball had been just three months in France, and already he had the reputation of being a first-class fighting airman. He was now flying one of the best machines yet produced by the Allies. It was a one-seater, and he had only his own life to think of and could therefore take chances which he would not have cared to take when he had another man with him. He was perfectly free to put himself against all Hun comers and he was thirsting for battle!

There was considerable activity in the air and behind the British lines. Tremendous work was being done in preparation for the great blow that was to send the Hun masses reeling back from their vast fortifications. Meanwhile, the German army was getting nearer to Verdun, and all the world was looking on breathlessly at the heroic defence of the French.

Ball says nothing in his letters about the mighty struggle that was impending, although he must have known of what was happening. The fact that his 'leave' was cancelled three times in almost as many weeks, and that on the third occasion he was actually on his way home when he was called back, shows how critical were those days, and also how valuable his services had already become. Every day he was flying over the lines looking down upon the scarred and cratered landscape where shortly hundreds of thousands of men were to engage in one of the most bloody conflicts of the war. We know little of the work

Ball was doing, but we do know that wonderful work was being done by the British squadrons supplying the vital information which was to guide the British Command in the plans they were making for the great offensive. Desperate efforts were made by the enemy machines to interrupt the methodical surveys of the German lines that were going on hour by hour, day after day, whenever weather conditions permitted, but the operations of our squadrons were never seriously hindered, although there were heavy losses inevitable in dangerous work of the kind.

As a scout pilot, Ball was one of the expert flyers whose duty it was to engage the fast enemy machines that were trying to swoop down upon and destroy the slower moving aeroplanes at work photographing the German trenches and spotting for our artillery.

At the end of May he had four fights in one patrol, and it is clear from the following letter that the Air command were beginning to take unusual notice of his work:

Well, I have been before General Higgins again for a stunt I had on May 29th [he says].

I had four fights in one patrol on my Nieuport, and came off top in every fight. Four Fokkers and an L.V.G. attacked me about 12 miles over the lines. I forced the L.V.G. down with a drum and a half, after which I zoomed up after the Fokkers. They ran away at once.

Out of all the fights I only got about 8 shots into my machine, one just missed my back and hit the strut. However, on my way back, the Hun Archie guns hit the tail of my machine and took a piece away, but I got back and have now got a new tail. The other fights were with Albatross machines. General Higgins sent for me on landing, and was very pleased.

Well, my garden is going on fine, peas are now about four inches, and I had the first crop of mustard and cress in the mess yesterday. It did make the chaps laugh, but they liked it.

I have just spent half-an-hour spring-cleaning my tent. Oh, it has been a big job. You see, I have no servant, for I live on the aerodrome, and the mess is about two miles away.

Three days later he described an adventure he had over a Hun aerodrome, where he deliberately challenged the Hun airmen to come up and fight.

I am now in my tent writing this letter. It is very hot, and my garden is coming on fine. I have got my cucumber and marrow plants well up, and doing well.

Am very happy to-day, for I had another good scrap yesterday until they sent machines up after me. I had to wait half-an-hour, but at last I was rewarded by seeing an Albatross and a Fokker being brought out. They were soon out and up. I went for the Albatross first, when it was 10,000 up. Put a drum into it, after which it dived back into the aerodrome, having had enough. During this, the Fokker had gone round in the rear and was sneaking up behind my tail. I waited until it was a few yards off, and had opened fire, then turned round and chased. It was so surprised that it only gave me time to get three shots in. It was in such a hurry that it landed in a field, and would not go back to its aerodrome until I had gone.

General Higgins was again in our aerodrome when I came back, and was very pleased with life. I had two other chases, but nothing worth telling.

Well, enough shop, for it gets so beastly always talking about our life, but I know you like to be in the know.

It was not difficult to see from his letters what great risks he was running. No boy who so frankly expressed himself as Ball did could altogether disguise the danger, and his parents could not hide their anxiety from him either.

Fully conscious of the perils he and his comrades had to face, Ball did not seek to disabuse the minds of his people. In the following letter home, written on 5 June, just before he had his first leave, he asks them to 'take it well' should he fall:

If I am getting my leave on Monday next, June 12th, this will be my last letter. You must not let little things like this push the stuffing out of you. Why, this makes the third time my leave has been stopped. I even had my warrant last time and was on the way. But we cannot have all things. You see, I have the Scout, which in itself is a great gift. However, I am quite ready for home now. Oh! so many people are asking me to call on them when I do get leave – I shall have a time. Oh! the news that Cyril is on another month's leave nearly sent me mad. We will have a topping time – really, I am a lucky chap. If you are not well when I get home, I shall take you a ride on the back of my cycle; but if you are well, mother must ride in the side-car and you on the back. Now won't that be fine?

Re you saying that if anything happens to me, *if* anything did happen, as it quite easily may, I expect you and wish you to take it well, for men tons better than I go in hundreds every day. However, I will be careful, as you wish, but I do like my job, and this is a great help. My garden is going on fine. My peas are running up sticks now.

Tell Cill and Lol. that my tales will grow and stretch a little more each day, so they will be quite ripe when I do arrive.

This is the first time that Ball had let his home know that at any time the end might come to him as it might to all his comrades. There are not many homes in England that have not received similar messages. Ball knew very well what the chances were every time he went up, just as the infantryman realises what it means to 'go over the top.' His promise to be careful sounds pathetic now we know what risks he took and with what calm he faced the dangers that crowded about him every hour that he was flying over the enemy lines. His reference to the other better men who were going every day is characteristic of his modesty and fine feeling. Before he left France he sent another note home:

June 7th.

My Dearest Mother,

I expect to get into Nottingham Monday or Tuesday, that is if all goes well; if not, well, I have luck in other ways, for I have had twelve more fights than anyone in Nos. 4 and 13 Squadrons in the last three months. Also I am the only one of the Scout Pilots who has brought a Hun down since we formed the Scout Group. So I have had tons of luck. Well, I am going out to No. —'s dinner to-night, so must close.

A man who could consider himself lucky because he had had more fights than anybody else was an ideal soldier! 'Tons of luck' – what a phrase! And this was the spirit of the men whom the Huns were now challenging in a desperate endeavour to make Germany the greatest force in the air.

The spirit of comradeship among all ranks in the British Army was perhaps most conspicuous among the flying men. These boys were more than great friends – they were brothers. Ball delighted in the affection he felt for the men in his Squadron. He was constantly writing home in terms of admiration about them.

'Sergeant— has just been in to ask if the officers would subscribe towards a football for 'B' Flight,' he wrote to a friend. 'I have taken the chance of repaying the lads in a small way and have sent to Gamage's for a football for them. They are all toppers and work like slaves night and day.'

It will have been noticed that Ball makes an occasional reference to his garden and to the flourishing growth of certain flowers and vegetables he had planted there. It was early in the spring that he first turned his attention to the possibilities of cultivating a little plot of land round about his hut at the Aerodrome. During the bad weather he found the days rather wearisome, and to one who had always contrived to keep his mind fully occupied, it was a misery to slack about with nothing to do. Also it is evident that with all his joy in flying and his ardour for battle, he realised that the nervous strain would be very great, and that so long as he was on earth the more he took his mind off the business of flying and fighting the better it would be for his health and for his efficiency as a pilot.

So as with everything else, he took up gardening with enthusiasm, and he wrote home about his plans:

No flying on account of the rain …

One of our men is putting a wire round the tent, making a space of about 40 square yards.

This is being turned into a garden, in which I hope to spend my spare time in the evenings.

Will you do me the great favour of sending me one packet of marrow seeds, one of lettuce, one of carrots, and a good big packet of mustard and cress. Also I would like a few flower seeds, one packet of sweet peas, and also a few packets of any other flowers that will grow quickly. You will think this idea strange, but you see it will be a good thing to take my mind off my work, also I shall like it.

My work will be rather a nerve pull, so I think it is best for me to forget all about it after it is over.

I have had my tent put on my job, for it is placed on the Aerodrome. This will be nice, for if ever a Hun comes I shall always be on the good work at once. The Mess is about three miles away, but the walk will do me good.

Please give my love to Lol and Cill, and tell them I am at last in for the *real work*.

112

A few days later a rainy day gave him a good innings in his allotment. On 13 May he wrote:

> I got up at 6 a.m. It was raining, so I could not fly. However, I got my tools and set to work on my garden, for rainy days are just right for setting seeds. In three hours I just managed to dig a piece of ground 12 ft. by 6 ft. In this I planted *Green Peas*. I hope to get in a few rows of beans to-morrow, if I have time to dig up another piece of ground.
>
> After this I boiled a bucket of water on a fire outside my tent. Had a wash and complete change, and now my tent is full of chaps wishing to hear the gramophone.

A homely description of the hut he built on the aerodrome and of his little garden is given by a sergeant in the Corps:

> A dinky little affair built up from old packing cases and odd pieces of lumber – a standing example to his perseverance. His little garden was an example of splendid taste, everything just so. Then the gramophone spoke of home and peace, of friends, mother and dad. He would be enjoying the happy task of arranging the small plants, and, perhaps, planning for the younger plants, when, without a moment's warning, he would issue the order that such and such a machine was in such and such a place. Then the real pluck and courage of a lion would assert itself, and many a pair of admiring eyes would follow the direction of his machine and often look in the direction long after the machine was out of sight. His was a splendid courage – a splendid temperament.

A wonderful memory this – of a boy one moment happy in a garden of his own making, enthusing over the growth of vegetables that were subsequently to be served in the Mess, and another moment careering through the air chasing and killing Germans.

Captain Ball and his canine friend.

CHAPTER 8

'With God's Help'

On 10 June Albert Ball came home on his first leave. In his simple, happy way of enjoying himself he made the most of it. He was back again in France on the 22nd. The note he wrote just before embarking, read in conjunction with his next letter from the front, makes one feel how precarious his life was:

Dearest Mother and Dad [he wrote from Folkestone],
Just a line before leaving dear old England again. You have been dears during my leave. Well now, dears, I will not attempt a long letter, for the boat goes soon. I shall do my best during the time I am away, also when I come back, shall try, with God's help, to repay your dear love.

In his very next letter, dated 27 June, he opens with the casual intelligence that he has just escaped being 'done in.'

Dearest Mother and Dad,
I have only just missed being done in to-day. I was on the 7 o'clock patrol to-day and on my patrol I saw over the lines a lot of transports, &c., in a wood. I went over the lines in order to have a good look, so that I could report the place, but the old Huns did not like it. They surrounded us with shells from their Archie guns, and at last we were hit. One of my cylinders was smashed off, also the machine got a few through it. One only

just missed my leg. However, the engine stopped, but I saw what I went to see, and also managed to get my machine far enough over our lines to prevent the-old fools from shelling it. Later on I had a new engine put in and the machine patched up, and it is now safely in the shed. Tomorrow the major is going to let me have my own back, for he has arranged for a shoot tomorrow, and we will not leave the place until every stone is smashed up. It was really good sport, and so we want them to have a little of the same kind of sport. I am sending half of the cylinder to you.

Well, you dears, although I would like to write for a year I cannot do so, for I have another job on now.

All is A1 and I am very happy.

But all was not exactly A1 for long.

Just about the time Ball left for his short leave, the great bombardment of the German lines on the Somme had commenced, and he returned a few days before the grand assault on a twenty-five mile front was launched. He therefore dived right into the thick of the hottest fighting in the air since the war began. The Germans, expecting a powerful offensive somewhere along the front, were sending out formidable formations in a determined effort to find out what was going on behind our lines, where there was the greatest activity.

It was the duty of Ball and his comrades to blind the eyes of the enemy so as to keep them in the greatest suspense and uncertainty. That they did this with considerable success was proved by the fact that when the attack began, the Germans were taken by surprise on at least one important and extensive sector.

Their aeroplanes were, however, not the only eyes the Germans had in the air. Keeping observation of the lines were a large number of sausage balloons guarded from aeroplane attacks by every device the enemy could employ. These balloons are not so vulnerable as they look, but thanks to the daring and skill of our pilots, very many of them were destroyed.

One of Ball's first exploits on his return to France was in a big concerted attack on some of these balloons. That it was a very dangerous and difficult operation will be seen from the following letter:

June 28th.

My Dearest Mother and Dad,

You will really begin to think that I am never going to send you a few lines. Am so sorry, but we have been up to our eyes in work since I arrived. You see, we only have four Scout Pilots left, out of eight. Poor old Captain C— was killed on my machine during my leave. He had only just come back from leave.

Lieutenant A—'s leg is smashed in five places. Lieutenant C— is in bed, etc., etc. So you see, we have tons of work to do.

You will have seen in the papers that on the 26th five German balloons were brought down. I brought one of them down, and at night a wire came from General Trenchard and General Higgins, congratulating me.

Oh! it was rotten, for I only just got back. Three of us were sent from this squadron. The first time we did no good, so I asked for another chance. We all set out again. I went for my balloon and set it on fire, but my engine was badly hit, and I had to come back all the eight miles over Hun land, at half speed, and only a few feet up. My machine was hit badly. I have enclosed one of the bullets. This bullet went through my induction pipe, engine bearer plate and three inches of wood. Not so bad, is it?

The other chaps were not very successful. One crashed his machine and the other did no good. The other four balloons were brought down by other squadrons. Five were brought down by the R.F.C. About one hundred machines went up for different balloons, so I think five is quite a good average for such a rotten job. You see, we had to get so low.

117

Well, enough of the above. I am building a hut in my spare time, for my tent is so damp. My garden is doing fine. The peas are now up four feet.

Now time is short, so I will not attempt a long letter.

It was for this achievement, following upon other brilliant work, that he was awarded the Military Cross. He was then a second lieutenant of the 7th Battalion Notts. and Derbyshire Regiment Territorial Force and of the Royal Flying Corps. The award was announced in the *London Gazette* dated 27 July 1916.

The official description of his achievement read: 'For conspicuous skill and gallantry on many occasions – notably when after failing to destroy an enemy kite balloon with bombs, he returned for a fresh supply, went back and brought it down in flames.'

Ball acquired a habit of 'going back' when he had not attained his object. Often he would return to the aerodrome with a machine riddled with shot – the pieces barely holding together – obtain another machine and enter the fray again. On the occasion of the first assault on the enemy balloon all his bombs missed. All the time he was subjected to a heavy and accurate anti-aircraft fire, and the enemy gunners had a good target because he had to remain poised at a low altitude directly over the balloon in order to drop his bombs with any prospect of scoring a hit.

Only airmen can realise what it means to fly 8 miles over the enemy lines at half speed and only a few feet up. Ball never had a narrower escape from capture or destruction than this. It was a great day's work, and his efforts at this time must have had a great influence on the development of the operations on this particular part of the front.

Ball told his father about the Military Cross in a letter which shows what strenuous days he and his comrades were spending:

Oh, yes, I bet you think that you are never going to have another letter [he wrote], but it is only luck, or at least bad luck, that I am able to get a few seconds off now.

My Nieuport engine has just gone poo-poo, so I have not got anything to fly until a.m. to-morrow morning. The men will work all night and have a new engine in by 2.0 a.m. in the morning.

The three Nieuport machines stand from a.m. until 9.30 at night, so you bet we are getting a rotten time just now. However, things are looking good just now, so we might all help and keep things going at any cost. But it is a long day and I am afraid that if it lasts very long, a few of the chaps will be going sick.

You will be pleased to hear that I have now got my Military Cross. I received the wire from the Wing yesterday, also congratulations from the Army Commander.

In a few weeks I get four days leave, in order to be decorated by the dear old King. Oh! I am so very pleased, for it has been a rotten job getting it. I cannot say exactly when I shall get the four days, for we have so much work to do just now, that one cannot get off, but I will come first chance I get.

I was given the ribbon by the Major to-day. The Cross I shall give to you, in order that you may keep it for me.

Well, enough about the M.C., for I do not want to bore you, and I must now close, for I have heaps to do.

It will be noticed that Ball makes no reference to the tremendous events that were about to take place, but it is pretty obvious that a great strain was being put on the energies of the flying men. This last letter was written on 1 July, one date that will forever stand out in the history of the campaign of the Western Front. It was on that day the news came that the great offensive had begun and the thrilling message came through, 'All goes well.'

Tens of thousands of the best of the man-hood of the Empire sprang over the parapets on that day to capture the subterranean fortresses that the Germans thought to be impregnable and to perish in the terrible machine gun fire that had to be encountered. Our losses in the air were also inevitably heavy, but the Huns were well beaten there also and lost more than we did.

To his mother he wrote on 1 July:

> Hello, my own, and how are you? I am O.K., but oh! so fagged. However, I shall soon get over that. Things are on full steam just now, 2.30 a.m. until 9.30 p.m. Well, now, I won't repeat my news, for I am simply up to my eyes in work and I know you will not expect it just now.
>
> Am so pleased to hear from your last very sweet letter that all is well.
>
> Well, now you will excuse this very short letter, won't you?
>
> P.S. – Thanks so much for chocs. I have just received them. They are O.K.
>
> P.S. – Am just going up to test Nieuport, 6.0. p.m.

From 2.30 a.m. until 9.30 p.m.! That was a tremendous strain, but the armies were pushing through the enemy lines and it was imperative not only to keep into touch with them until our own lines of communication had been brought up, but also to be continually harassing the enemy in his preparations for counter-attacks. It would be light early in the morning with a very long stretch before darkness fell, and it meant many flights before the brief rest came.

Ball was now a famous airman.

His reputation was known in the British Army and had spread beyond it to the French, but England as yet knew nothing about him. The award of the Military Cross did not let the public into the secret that the Army was talking about a wonderful boy-airman who had accounted for six enemy machines and one balloon. The Royal Flying Corps does not court publicity. Ball certainly did not. In one letter written in this month of July he said: '*Re* the newspapers saying anything about me. If they put in any bosh I shall be more than wild. If they just say that I downed five machines and a balloon all well and good, but nothing else. I like doing things but I don't like big songs about them.'

These letters home were private and their contents were known to a very small circle.

His letters dated 3, 4 and 6 July, however, disclose that Ball had a great many admirers, and that the Army Command were watching him with great appreciation.

July 3rd and 4th.

My Dearest Mother and Dad,
Only ten minutes, so my letter must just consist of latest news.

Yesterday, 2nd, I brought down two Hun machines in flight; and at night received another wire from Army Commander congratulating me.

To-day I am trying for a balloon. I now stand with six machines and one balloon to my credit. No one else in the squadron has got more than one. However, their time of luck will come.

So long, dears.

P.S. – M. Le Pri sent a letter asking me to put my name in his autograph book yesterday. He is the great French flying man, and has brought down ten machines.

July 6th.

My Dear Old Dad,
Thanks so much for your congratulations. Since the balloon stunt I have been given the M.C. and also on July 2nd brought down two more Huns. General Trenchard again has sent me a wire congratulating me, also he came up to our aerodrome and repeated his words. Also General Higgins saw me again and was very pleased with life.

I am repeating the above news in this letter, for I am afraid that the letter that I wrote on the 3rd must have gone *west*.

Hereabouts Ball wrote some of his most interesting letters. He had now established a great reputation and was doing big things almost every day. But there was no sign of over confidence or any suggestion that he was inclined to under-rate the powers of his opponents. He was, in fact, by no means satisfied with the machine he was flying, and also he was losing many comrades who went to their death on the Somme battles. A letter written on 10 July to his sister shows that the German airmen were making a hard fight of it:

> I am really so sorry that I have been so long in writing, but you will understand what things are like out here just now. Really one has only just time to button up one's tunic. However, so far have managed that.
>
> I am having a very poo-poo time, but most interesting. On the 6th three topping chaps went off and never returned. Yesterday four of my best pals went off and to-day one of our new chaps has gone over, so you can guess we are always having to get used to new faces.
>
> I am coming home in a few days for my visit to Buckingham Palace, and I shall have four days at home.
>
> I am working on my machine to-day, for it is very dud, but I hope to have all O.K. to-night.
>
> Oh! well, dear, you must excuse this very short letter, for I must now get on with my work.

It was a wonder that Ball survived those anxious days. He marvelled at his own escapes and could only attribute it in part to a Divine influence.

CHAPTER 9

'Why I Feel Safe'

Re saying a few words to God when I am doing my work and when it is done. You ask me if I did when I came back safely. You bet I did. I even do when I am fighting; in fact, I put all my trust in God, that is why I feel safe, no matter in what mess I get.

Well, I am having topping luck and happiness in every direction.

July 10th, 1.20 p.m.

My Dear Dad,

Have just received your letter, and very pleased I am, for I am feeling a poo-poo crock to-day. All the machines are going rotten just now, and we keep losing a lot. Yesterday, four of my great pals went out and never came back. One of them was brought down by anti-aircraft, and was on fire.

I went up this morning after three Huns and managed to get underneath them, but could not get nearer than 3,000 ft. owing to my engine. It was rotten luck; however, I am spending the remainder of the day trying to get it right, so I hope to-night to have a good machine ready to carry on with the good work.

You ask me to let the devils have it when I fight. Yes, I always let them have all I can, but really I don't think them devils. I only scrap because it is my duty, but I do not think anything bad about the Hun. He is just a good chap with very little guts, trying to do his best. Nothing makes me feel more rotten than to see them go down, but you see it is either them or me, so I must do my best to make it a case of *them*.

You ask me if it will be long before you can address my letters any other than 2nd Lieut. Oh, I never rush round trying to get promotions. All I want is plenty of good work to do. I am very satisfied.

We have put at the head of this chapter these two extracts from Albert Ball's correspondence because they are a revelation of a side of his character of which very few people could have been aware. It will be an inspiration to many in these days of tragedy to know that the boy who slew so terribly did not rejoice in the death of his enemy even though they were Huns, and that there was a spirituality in his nature which ennobled those combats in the air – fierce and merciless as they were.

It is true that he once wrote: 'Oh, don't you trouble about me being afraid to acknowledge God before people. I shall never neglect that duty'; but the young pilots who knew him well never suspected that Ball gave a thought to the religious faith in which he was nurtured. They were impressed by his striking sense of duty to his country. They say that he seemed to be conscious of a special responsibility, of a power to do a great service to his country which was greatly needed. His irresponsibility, his rarely failing light-heartedness could not conceal the serious purpose, the earnest desire to do all he could to help to save England. In a letter which is given later on in this chapter, he says to his father: 'You ask me to be sure to come back safely. Oh, yes, if God wishes it, I shall come back safely, and, oh, I do want to, but I want to get a few more scraps yet, for one must stick at it.'

Ball several times wrote as if he felt that there was a Divine influence watching over him, protecting him when he was flying.

The airman poet, Paul Bewsher, has written of a similar belief in 'The Dawn Patrol'.

Then do I feel with God quite quite alone,
High in the virgin morn, so white and still,
And free from human ill:
My prayers transcend my feeble earth-bound plaints –
As though I sang among the happy Saints
With many a holy thrill –
As though the glowing sun were God's bright Throne.

My flight is done. I cross the line of foam
That breaks about a town of grey and red,
Whose streets and squares lie dead
Beneath the silent dawn – then am I proud
That England's peace to guard I am allowed –
Then bow my humble head,
In thanks to Him Who brings me safely home.

Ball believed in the power of prayer. A favourite prayer of his was one selected from a volume of Prayers, written at Vailima, by Robert Louis Stevenson, and especially this passage which he often said in France: 'Grant me courage to endure the lesser ills unshaken, to accept death, loss, disappointment, as it were straws upon the tide of life.'

His motto was *Nil Sine Deo*.

Some of the spoken and printed descriptions about him in these days are worth quoting.

Thus a sergeant is reported as speaking of his 'extraordinary courage and eagerness to attack the enemy which set up a noble example. A white puff high up over the lines was sufficient for him, and whether early dawn or late on in the evening he was eager to encounter a hostile machine. It was nothing unusual to see him climbing into his machine in his pyjamas.'

A brother officer who was in the same squadron with Ball for some time said:

I got a very good idea of what the man was. Plenty of people who know nothing about it make him out to be a wonderful flyer who was always up to star stunts. But there was really nothing of that about Ball at all. Never for one moment was he what flying men call a star performer. He knew less tricks than many novices, and he never once 'swanked' in the air. He was never a fancy pilot, but always a very great man. He was grit and fight, fight and grit, first, last, and all the time.

'He was absolutely fearless but never reckless,' said another comrade. 'He realised that a good airman ought not to throw away uselessly the lives of himself or others, but where there was a reasonable chance of doing good work, danger never deterred him. For the Allies' cause he was ready to dare anything.'

Ball at one time felt the strain of continuous flying and fighting so much that he was troubled lest he should not be able to keep up the reputation as a first-class fighting man.

During July 1916 he was on the verge of a breakdown, but the great British offensive was then in full swing, and every airman who could fly and fight was badly wanted: 'Yesterday I was up at 5 a.m.,' he wrote on 6 July, 'and during the day had twelve flights, but at last nature is asking to have its own way. However, I am not done yet. I shall get at them again soon.'

He took a short rest which, however, did not mean giving up flying altogether.

July 18th.

My Dear Dad,

The day before yesterday we had a big day. At night I was feeling very rotten, and my nerves were poo-poo. Naturally, I cannot keep on for ever, so at night I went to see the C.O., and asked him if I could have a short rest, and not fly for a few days. He said he would do his best.

What has taken place has been that I have been sent to No. 8 Squadron, back on to B.E. 2.c.'s. Oh, I am feeling in the dumps.

July 20th.

Dearest Mother and Dad,

Hello, all is well again, for I am well on the way to being O.K.

Last night Captain P— came back from leave. He has got a Flight in this Squadron. I asked him to get me in. his Flight, and he did it at once, so after all things are not so bad.

My old Majors of No. 11 and No. 13 have gone to the trouble of writing very nice letters to the C.O. of this Squadron.

Major— of No. ix, wrote:— 'You will find Ball a good little chap if managed in the right way. He is young, so naturally wants a little more rope than the older pilots, etc., etc.'

He has also enclosed a list of my fights on the Bristol and Nieuport, also the five machines and balloon I brought down. He ends up by saying that if I am feeling like coming back after a few weeks with No. 8, he will be only too pleased to have me.

I am advised to have my change here, and then to ask to go back, stating at the same time that I have had enough rest. It is anything but a rest here, for the machines are so rotten and slow, but it will do me good. Yesterday I only did two flights, a patrol at 4 a.m. and a bombing raid at 12 p.m., so perhaps it is the best thing. Well, I will not grumble, but will play up and get well again. I must have been getting on too well for it to last, as I have had so much good luck.

Two days later he reported that all was well again, and volunteered for a very dangerous job. He wrote on 25 July: 'I am going back to my old squadron in a few days, but first I have promised to do a job, or at least try to do a job for this squadron. It is a rotten job, and one that has often been tried without success, but, if God helps me in His usual way, I shall pull it off.'

It was a self-appointed task, as the following shows: 'I heard of it and asked for the job. The C.O. asked the General if I could do if, and at first he said 'No,' but yesterday he said I could try, so, the first good chance I get, the Ball will have another run. If this is successful I shall run slow for a time, as my nerves are not quite what they were.' But the job had to be done first, the brave little airman decided.

'All is O.K. now,' he wrote two days later, 'I have got my second pip coming' – otherwise his second star or promotion to a full lieutenant. 'I have managed to get a good job – aforementioned – which, if it comes off, will be fine. However, lets pull it off first before talking about it,' he adds, practically.

'Something attempted, something done' was the order of things described in a letter dated 31 July 1916:

> The General came to the aerodrome on the 29th, and congratulated me on doing the job I mentioned in my previous letter. Yesterday we did two bombing raids. On the first one I had to lead, for the Wing Commander had to land owing to engine trouble. It was great sport as thirty machines went. On the second, it was more sport still. Three Fokkers came for us, but we did the job O.K., and set the place on fire. However, you will think I am a very bloodthirsty chap just now, but I am not really.

It seems that public attention was first drawn to the achievements of Ball by the French Press, who referred to him as the wonderful boy whose doings were the talk of both armies. 'A young British airman,' said one paper, 'has a record which surpasses even that of Maxine Lenoir, who has received the Legion of Honour ... he is Lieut. Albert Ball, the son of a former Mayor of Nottingham. He has taken part in 84 air-fights, and has brought down 22 enemy aeroplanes ...' *Le Journal* said: 'It is in aviation where we are equalled by the quickly formed army of the most sportive nation in the world. Lieut. Albert Ball has struck and brought down his 22nd aeroplane ... the young victor has been engaged in 84 air battles, and one night attacked by four enemy machines, he brought them all down. This new 'ace' of English aviation is only 19 years of age.'

Another paper pointed out later on in the year that like Nungesser, Ball destroyed three machines in one morning.

'Our heroes of the air are not named in the official communications until they have brought down their fifth aeroplane,' said *Le Miroir*. 'The British aviator Ball had accounted for more than 20 before he knew the honours of popularity ...'

> We possess in France a nomenclature of our flying men, but our English Allies shroud the doings of their heroes under a veil of anonymity. Notwithstanding, Captain Ball is not quite unknown to us. He is a remarkable pilot who bears favourable comparison with our greatest and best. His exploits have been awarded by the honours he deserves. – *Sporting*, Paris.

'We do not turn the limelight on our men,' said Mr. Price Bell, the doyen of American correspondents in London, 'but we could show plenty of Immelmanns if we did, perhaps super Immelmanns.' Said the *Daily Mail*, 'No courage could surpass that of the British airman, who flies within a few feet of the German trenches, when a shot in his petrol tank means death ... There are champions such as Lieut. Ball, who has already shot down 28 German machines, and once attacked twelve German aeroplanes single-handed.'

CHAPTER 10

The Red Battle Flyer

Lieut. Ball's machine could be distinguished from the others by a 'red spinner,' as he called it, fixed on the front of his propeller. This was his identification plate, a kind of bonnet painted red, which made it easy for observers in the air and on the ground to recognise who the pilot was. One advantage of wearing this mark was there could be no doubt when he brought down an enemy machine as to who did it. Sometimes after a flight Ball would go back to the aerodrome and another man would fly out to the spot indicated on the map in order to obtain corroborative evidence that the enemy machine was really destroyed.

It is said that when the German flyers saw the red nosecap coming in their direction they knew it was Ball, and preferred to keep out of his way.

'He is our star fighting flyer,' said one of his comrades, 'he has the admiration of all the lot of us. He is a short little chap, with longish black hair, and eyes like a hawk. Not many German machines come across our lines nowadays, for if they are anywhere near our friend he is up like a shot. And often he does not trouble to put on his tunic, but goes to battle in his shirt sleeves.'

The following are some fairly reliable accounts of some of his fights:

Observing a flock of seven hostile aeroplanes in formation, he engaged the foremost without hesitation. Getting to within

15 yards' range, he succeeded in forcing the machine down. The leader being 'crashed,' the remaining machines thereupon took to flight.

A little later seeing five enemy machines, he attacked one of them at less than a dozen yards and brought it down in flames. He then attacked the second machine which had been raining shots at him. After a brief duel the German 'was knocked out' of action. This second machine fell into a village and landed on the top of a house, and was smashed to pieces.

By this time Ball had run out of ammunition, so he called at the nearest aerodrome for more, and having taken in fresh supplies started off for his next victim.

His next 'stunt' was a fight with three hostile machines, all of which he caused to dive out of control, although his own plane was damaged with shot. This time he had to go back for more petrol!

On one special expedition he observed four Hun planes in formation. Without any preliminary manoeuvring he swooped down upon them and broke up the formation. He shot down the nearest machine which crashed down upon its 'proboscis.' Not being certain that this machine was properly smashed up he flew down to satisfy himself and found that the machine was hopelessly wrecked.

One of his most famous achievements was a fight with a dozen of the enemy. They were flying in formation, and Ball dived into the lot of them and emptied a drum into the nearest and put it out of action. The others came forward and met with a hot reception. Down went another one. Ball's machine was riddled with bullets and considerably damaged otherwise, but he succeeded in getting home unhurt. Nothing would probably have been known about this fight but for the report of another officer, in charge of an anti-aircraft battery who sent in an account describing how one British aeroplane attacked twelve German. Ball himself had said nothing at all about it.

In August 1916, Ball was promoted to full Lieutenant. In this month and in September during the continuation of the great offensive on the Western front, Ball and his comrades were doing magnificent work. He was one of a group of flyers whose total for September included fifty German machines definitely brought down, sixty hit under difficult conditions, six Drachens burnt, making a total for the three months of 123 machines destroyed, and 114 seriously damaged and suffering a more or less disastrous fate. All this was, of course, apart from the great raids behind the German lines in which thousands of tons of bombs were dropped.

On 30 August he wrote to his sister:

Dearest Little Girl,
Am so sorry that I have been so long in answering your letter, but what with changing squadrons and flying, etc., I have really been unable to write much. However, it is raining to-day, so I am letter-writing.

We are going to my old aerodrome to-morrow, so I shall again be in my dear old hut. You will be pleased to hear that I have now got more Huns to my credit than any English or French pilot. The Major asked for a list to-day, and it worked out:—
84 combats.
11 Hun machines and one balloon brought down and seen to crash.
5 Hun machines brought down but not seen to crash.
12 forced down and damaged.
So it is not so bad, and I have done my best.

Ball began September well by adding two more German machines to his credit. He was awarded the Distinguished Service Order.

'Got two Huns out of twelve last night,' he said, 'was shot down, but am not hurt. Have been awarded D.S.O.'

The day before he left France on short leave – 2 September – was the date when he engaged a fleet of between twenty and thirty Hun machines, and when he brought down four Huns before he himself came down. This was the occasion when his ammunition ran out and he killed the pilot of one of the enemy machines.

On the official report of this great achievement being made to the Commander-in-Chief General Sir Douglas Haig wrote on the statement: '*Well done.—D. H.*'

By this time Ball was recognised as the supremely brilliant airman of the war. When he got his DSO, congratulations came from all quarters, from the Allied airmen, from his friends at home, and from unknown friends in America. He was certainly regarded in France as the unrivalled airman of the British Army. The achievements of Captain Boelcke, the German airman, as recorded in the German Press with or without exaggeration, certainly could not compare with what Ball had done. So far as the total victims was concerned, they were apparently level, twenty each; this was also the total of the brilliant Frenchman, Lieut. Nungesser.

Boelcke's record was soon left far behind by Ball. Up to 22 September 1916, he had established the record of having completely destroyed in air fights 23 enemy aeroplanes, and he was rapidly adding to the total. His letters reflected some of his elation: 'Well, I have been having a bit of luck in the last week.'

He wrote on 13 August:

On Monday last I had dinner with the Colonel. On Wednesday, August 9th, I attacked a balloon with a B.E., and forced the observer to jump out (this was mentioned in the Army report, also in a special report to the wing). On the way back from this job, my main spar and wing tip was crashed, but we got back to the aerodrome. Lieut. H— was my observer.

On Saturday, August 12th, I attacked an Albatross without my observer and forced him down. To finish the week I got tons of chocolate and letters from you and Mother.

Not a bad week for B.E.'s, is it? Oh, but I shall be glad to get back to my Nieuport. I shall be pleased when I get home. Have to go up now.

August 14th.

Hello, I was unable to finish this yesterday, so I will continue now. First of all, let me thank you for the kind gift you sent me. I was surprised to hear that it was my birthday, and, oh, it is a happy one. Major H— has just rung up to say that I am to return to my squadron. He finished up by saying that he had got a brand new machine for me. So you bet I shall be able to get my own back now. And won't it be O.K. to see my garden again? Do you know that if I had not been sent to this squadron I should have been a Flight by now and my three pips. However, I shall not be long getting them, for I am out for it.

I think it has done me good being here, for I now know artillery work and bombing. All this helps to make a good flying officer.

Thanks so much for your kind wishes. Oh, don't you trouble about me being afraid to acknowledge God before people. I shall never neglect that duty.

August 14th.

Dearest Little Mother,

Oh, I am in a mess, for I have tons of letters to write, and really don't know which end to start first.

You ask if my hut garden will be A1. Oh, yes, I have a gardener to see after it during the time I have been away. He often sends peas, etc., over to me at No. 8.

Well, I am going back to my hut to-night, so I'll soon be out again. Won't it be A1.

So cheero.

August 16th.

Dearest People,

Hello, am back again in my dear old hut. All is O.K., and my garden is fine. You will be surprised to hear that I have started with luck. I went up this morning and attacked five Hun machines. One I got and two I forced down. After this I had to run, for all my ammunition was used. However, I got back O.K., with only two hits on my machine.

I have got one of the latest Nieuports, and, oh, it is nice to be without a passenger again. Well, now I have only a few seconds, so I must close soon. I am on full steam again and hope to do tons of work.

Please send me as much stuff like tinned meats, etc., as you like, for I now have mess on the aerodrome in my hut in order to be on the job all the time.

With his Nieuport Ball was now very happy, and flying and fighting at the top of his form.

Cheerio! Am so sorry that I have been such an age without writing you a line, but work has been on all sides, so it had to come first [he wrote on 20 August, announcing that he was acting as Flight-Commander].

I am acting Flight-Commander just now, so have many little jobs to do. The real flight C.O. is on leave. Well, it is a dud morning, so we are not doing much flying. This is my chance to get in a lot of letters.

I received your very topping pudding a few days ago. It was O.K. All the chaps thought so, and you bet I did.

In this same letter there is one very interesting injunction about his decoration:

Re addressing my letters Lieut, and M.C., I have been recommended for my second pip, but it is not through yet (M.C. is not put at the end of my name, only V.C. if you manage to get it).

I will just tell you what I am doing, and how goes life out here. My hut and garden are very topping just now. I am writing this letter in my hut with the door wide open. It is O.K.

I think all the scouts are going into No. 60 Squadron before long. If this is so I shall go with them, but they may come here, so I shall only change my squadron and not my hut.

All is O.K. Must close now. Am just off up after a Hun.

August 22nd.

My Dearest Dad,

This is the second letter I have written for you this morning. The first one I have just put on the fire, for it was so short and uninteresting. Yesterday I was up eight times. Had two fights but only succeeded in making the machines run, for I could not get quite near enough, they were so fast. To-day I have only been up once, but am off again soon. It is only 10 a.m.

In his next letter Ball told a wonderful story. It gives a striking indication of the ascendency he had achieved over the Huns. It is a letter full of fights and thrills, and it is surely one of the most astonishing messages a boy ever sent home:

My Dearest Mother and Dad,

Cheerio, dears. And, oh, the wind blows good out here. Do so hope it is the same with you.

Really, I am having too much luck for a boy. I will start straight away, and tell you all. On August 22nd I went up. Met twelve Huns.

No. 1 fight. I attacked and fired two drums, bringing the machine down just outside a village. All crashed up.

No. 2 fight. I attacked and got under machine, putting in two drums. Hun went down in flames.

No. 3 fight. I attacked and put in one drum. Machine went down and crashed on a housetop.

All these fights were seen and reported by other machines that saw them go down.

I only got hit eleven times in the planes, so I returned and got more ammunition. This time luck was not all on the spot. I was met by about 14 Huns, about 15 miles over their side. My wind screen was hit in four places, mirror broken, the spar of the left plane broken, also engine ran out of petrol. But I had good sport and good luck, but only just, for I was brought down about one mile over our side. I slept near the machine and had it repaired during the night.

This work was done while I was still in No. 11 Squadron. In the morning I flew over to No. 60 Squadron, and spent the 23rd and 24th in getting settled down. I had a short flight on the 24th but only chased one Hun.

The General came to me on the 24th and congratulated me. He said in fun, 'I am putting your name on a big board in the trenches in order to frighten the Huns.'

My C.O. rang up and told me that I am getting a flight C.O.'s job, so this means that I shall be a Captain. Oh, la la. Topping, isn't it? Well, this will come along in time; I think it a topping reward, don't you?

To-day is the 25th. And I have again been in for it. Three fights. Two machines I brought down, and one I crashed. Not so bad, four Huns in four days, is it? The Colonel came up to the aerodrome and congratulated me.

I have no more news of importance, and still less time to tell it, so I must now close.

Good-night, dears. All my love.

In a few days he wrote saying that he had again been reported dead – the explanation is amusing enough:

Hello, dear, how goes things? All is going much better with me to-day, although I was very much in the dumps yesterday.

Last night I had three more fights and crashed one Hun machine to earth.

I was again reported dead, for I went down after the Hun to make sure he was done in. However, I returned all right, so all is O.K.

A French Major called to congratulate me yesterday. He said I have now got more Huns than any French flying man. If that is so, I have got more than any pilot out in France, English or French. They make it out to be 16 crashed in 84 fights, also the balloon. But I think it is only 12 crashed and the balloon out of 84 fights.

The Major had a long talk with me to-day. He is very pleased, and says I may have leave, next but one. Also I shall be coming home for a long rest soon, and I really think that I shall get it. Oh, won't it be A1? I do so want to leave all this beastly killing for a time.

Well, I expect to be in my dear old hut before long, for I think we are going to the old aerodrome.

September 1st.

Dear Dad,

Got two Huns out of 12 last night. Was shot down, but am not hurt. Have been awarded D.S.O.

Will be on leave soon. Love.

Albert.

Some of the official accounts of Ball's flights which have been supplied make exciting reading.

In one report we read of S.E. 5a. 8898 (Leader), the official description of Ball's machine travelling north towards Cambrai with two other machines in order to view a southern aerodrome. A number of machines which appeared to be Albatross Scouts were observed leaving the ground. Eight Albatross Scouts of a similar type were also in the air. Ball dived at the nearest machine putting 'in a short burst of Vickers.' The Hun broke away but Ball hung on to his tail and fired a long burst of Vickers, eventually getting underneath and firing half a drum from Lewis gun at very close range, the Hun going down and crashing near Graincourt.

The German formation having scattered and made off towards Douai, Ball and another made off towards them and having climbed to 12,000 ft viewed the two Albatross wireless machines, 'always to be seen over Vitry at 4,000 ft.' Ball and his companion machine dived but were met half way by four new Red Albatross Scouts. They drove in, eventually getting on the tails of the Huns, Ball firing a burst of Vickers at one machine 'which immediately went down seemingly O.K.' The other Huns 'put their noses down and cleared.'

On another occasion Ball had just turned when a large number of various types of Albatross Scouts coloured red and two-seaters coloured white were seen coming down upon him over Beaumont, Ball being then at 6,000 ft. According to the report he 'twisted and turned, and engaged first one H.A. and then another, getting well on to the tails of two H.A. in sequence, both of which went down seemingly O.K.' Then both his guns jambed, but being the faster machine he was able to get home alright.

Another time some Huns were seen leaving the ground somewhere east of Cambrai, so Ball 'went and sat over Cambrai and waited until the Huns were about 6,000 ft. and dived at the nearest firing a drum of Lewis and about 50 rounds of Vickers at the same time at a range of about 20 yards. The Hun went down quite out of control and crashed in a wood north-east of Cambrai. Ball turned in order to go back to the lines but about this time five enemy machines had got round on the west side, so he fired and tried to get through but could not. Turning south-east with the Huns in pursuit Ball waited until one of the enemy had got well in front of the other and then suddenly turned; dived and 'firing Lewis and all rounds Vickers until right up to H.A.,' which burst into flames and crashed. The remaining enemy machines followed and got in a few hits, but Ball firing at the nearest, a single-seater scout with a very long tail and a sharp nose, sent it down, but it was 'all O.K.' Ball continued south-east until dark by which time the Huns had gone.

With two other machines at 14,000 feet Ball sighted six Huns over Cambrai at 13,000 feet going north-west. They dived in among them, and Ball got on the tail of one Albatross only to have a Hun on his. He turned and when the Hun dived, gave chase and crashed him near Marquion.

Crossing the lines Ball travelled north-east and met two Huns at 11,000 feet; one of them got on his tail, so he turned and eventually brought it down out of control, then he attacked the other one. He 'opened fire with Vickers gun and kept the trigger pressed, until the machines almost came into each other.' Ball's engine was hit and he was covered with oil. The engine kept up the revolutions but lost all oil pressure. No other Huns came along, so Ball went down to about 3,000 feet and saw both his opponents lying on the ground within 400 yards of each other completely wrecked. He went back towards the line and met two more of the enemy near Lens. Having only a very few rounds left and not being able to see through his sights because of the oil, he put his 'nose' down and went home.

Four Red Albatross Scouts were sighted at 13,000 feet going south between Douai and the line. Ball had one machine with him and he dived at the nearest, but had 'four or five H.A. scouts coming down on his tail. Ball turned, fastened on to the tail of H.A. and followed it down 2,000 feet, riddling H.A. meanwhile.' The machine diving into the earth in the rough ground between Halte and Vitry, Ball turned and climbed up and joined a scrimmage which was now taking place between a number of double-seater enemy machines, scouts and Sopwith

Scouts, Bristol fighters and B.E.'s. Ball attacked one which dived steeply and cleared and the melee gradually made towards Douai, the Huns being out-manoeuvred and yielding ground. Over Sailley, Ball attacked a white two-seater Albatross which hurtled down, but owing to the dusk its ultimate aim could not be observed.

In another fight near Cambrai, Ball completely wrecked an enemy machine, and after a comrade had been brought down uninjured, he sat above the clouds until the arrival of an enemy machine which he followed to within 500 ft. of the ground in the face of heavy antiaircraft fire. His control was shot away, and his machine got into a spin. Ball, therefore, says the official report, 'had to give up fight and return home on left elevator which had only the top wire left.'

CHAPTER 11

Ball's Methods

What was the secret of Ball's success? It is doubtful whether Ball knew himself. Courage above all things and absolute fearlessness. 'My favourite dodge is now well known to the Huns,' he once said, 'so I am not giving anything away when I tell you that when I get to close quarters I generally pretend that I am going to attack from above. The Hun gets ready to fire up at me as I pass over, and then I suddenly dive under his machine and if I am lucky I empty a drum into his petrol tank and down he goes.' The truth about the methods of Ball and his comrades is that they had no prescribed rules of scientific warfare. They were quicker to adapt themselves to circumstances of the moment than their opponents. The German temperament likes rules. It likes to carry out rigidly the rules of any game it has been trained in. That no doubt does very well in land warfare, but in the air where a man is entirely alone, and entirely dependent upon his own initiative, it is no good waiting for the order of a commander. Quick decision is everything. A happy-go-lucky spirit like Ball was therefore bound to score against an opponent less irresponsible.

Mr. Howard E. Coffin, the chairman of the United States Aircraft Board, has put this point of view in the *Saturday Evening Post*:

The German [he said] requires leadership; loves the feel of his comrade's elbow. He is hurt by discipline, not free to independent action. He has therefore lacked the dash as an airman that has characterised his antagonists. The temperament of the Latin, on the other hand, fits admirably into the scheme of things above the clouds. The Frenchman is an ideal operator of a fighting machine. He is quick and daring and resourceful. He has a dash that is beyond all others, and delights in directing his own exploits. The Italian has a similar dash and a similar Latin recklessness. He is a good flier. The Britisher is a good airman for a different set of reasons. He is above all a sportsman, and airplaning is the greatest sport since Adam.

Ball more than once said that most of his opponents seemed afraid to take risks. They rarely came to close quarters if they could help it. 'These Hun fellows,' he said, 'are brave, but most of them lack confidence. Whenever you dash straight for a Hun machine, it will be always the first to turn to avoid a collision. A dash like that generally flusters them ... But now and again you do meet a sporting Hun who will put up a good fight, and be prepared to chance his luck.'

When he was at home during his last leave, Ball, under persistent cross-examination, gave several descriptions of his fights. It was one of the rare occasions that he was persuaded to go thoroughly into details about his own work. He spoke with enthusiasm and humour about a protracted duel he had with an unknown German airman who proved to be his match on at least this occasion. They were alone together, so that the conditions were absolutely fair, and they went for each other for all they were worth. Each tried one favourite stratagem after another, only to be baulked by a counter move. They fired from above and below at various angles. They circled in endeavours to get on to each other's tails, but it was no good, neither man could get in a mortal blow.

'We kept on firing,' said Ball, 'until we had used up all our ammunition. There was nothing more to be done after that, so we both burst out laughing. We couldn't help it – it was so ridiculous. We flew side by side laughing at each other for a few seconds, and then we waived adieu to each other and went off. He was a real sport was that Hun.'

One secret of his success was of course his great confidence. Nevertheless, he once confided that he often felt 'nervous just before starting a flight'. He even confessed to feeling 'afraid of being killed'. The man to whom he made this confession could not help smiling, but Ball seemed to be quite serious about it and explained naively enough that sometimes the reason why he was so keen on killing his opponents was that he was afraid of being killed himself. A thrilling encounter was that one he had at very close quarters with a brave and persistent German. Ball's ammunition was all gone and the German seemed to have got him set, but with lightning decision Ball pulled out his revolver and shot the German through the head when their machines must have been almost touching.

To say that Ball was very original in his tactics, and that was the reason why he invariably destroyed his opponent, does not altogether explain why he was so good. After all, it was courage rather than subtle tactics which made the man attack single-handed a whole squadron of Hun machines sometimes to the number of fourteen. By doing that he repeatedly broke up enemy formations, but of course it was done at great personal risk, and one never heard of the German 'cracks', like Immelmann, Boelcke, or Richthofen, taking similar great risks. The reputations of these Germans were built up mostly by single-handed contests against inexperienced opponents. The Germans have always taken the air warfare much more seriously than our airmen, and that may be one reason why they are not so successful.

A brother officer has spoken about Ball's extraordinary judgment. Another man who saw a good deal of him flying and fighting said that his control of his machine was 'marvellous – most uncanny.'

Ball himself was always talking about his luck. In his letters home he sometimes marvelled at it. He could give no other explanation of the reason why when time after time his machine was shattered and the shrapnel and the bullets punctured everything except his body, he was never hit at all. He said himself that in all his flights he hardly sustained so much as a scratch.

On the subject of the German machines, Ball, as we have shown, learned to think very little of the Fokker.

'The Fokkers are out of date now,' he said, speaking in the autumn of 1916. 'You can finish a Fokker any time you see one,' he said, not boastingly – for he never boasted – but as if speaking of a truth which had become commonplace.

'The best German machine now,' he said, 'is a Roland. She is a two-seater, her guns fire backwards and forwards, and everywhere except below. That is why I always go underneath them.'

'Once entirely surrounded by a flock of Fokkers, he succeeded in dispersing them after a fierce fire.' Brief statements like this is all we know of this and many other battles he fought.

After making a reconnaissance he steered into a fleet of the enemy. Two of them succeeded in sandwiching him between them, one tackling him from above, the other from underneath, firing as hard as they could go.

Ball tried a favourite trick. He 'fell' rapidly, and getting right under the lower Hun – a two-seater – fired five rounds and sent it down in flames. The observer was seen to climb out of the seat and leap clear of the flames.

Nobody more keenly appreciated the sporting spirit, the feeling of mutual respect that has existed between the airmen of both forces than Ball. He frequently spoke of 'a real sport' he had met, and never spoke of the German airmen in terms of hatred.

'He was a real sporting Hun and I should have been sorry had I killed him, and I think he would have been sorry, too, had he finished me off,' said Ball, speaking of the famous fight already mentioned, in which after fighting half-an-hour and exhausting their ammunition with no decisive result, he and the German burst out laughing and flew side by side before parting.

Altogether he was 'brought down' half a dozen times in the first six months of his fighting, generally with his engine smashed, but was always able to land without a crashing.

CHAPTER 12

'In England – Now'

When Ball came home on what proved to be his last leave, he was a national hero. Preparations had been made to give him a great civic welcome. But he contrived to arrive in the city almost unobserved and to go straight to his home, where he hoped to spend a quiet time among his own people. Ball, however, inevitably became the centre of many celebrations. He was entertained to lunch by the Mayor (Councillor Small), who said that his exceptional resources, ingenuity combined with his conspicuous gallantry, had placed him on a pedestal, and it was the intention of Nottingham to recognise his merits with the highest honour it was at the disposal of the city to confer. Ball's speech consisted of two sentences. In fact, he gave the assembled company more smiles than words. 'It is indeed kind of the Mayor to say such jolly decent things about me.'

'Take your time, my lad,' said a venerable alderman, seeking to give the nervous boy confidence. 'I think I shall have to,' Ball said in an aside, and then, 'I feel more than pleased to think that I have done something for my town.'

That was all that Albert Ball, the terror of the German airmen, had to say to the distinguished citizens of Nottingham who had come together to hear his story.

To the Mayor and the Sheriff he presented photographs, the frames of which were made from the tips of propellers of a

German aeroplane brought down by him in September. 'It came down in flames,' said Ball, 'and the poor devils in it were both killed, but that was better than our fellows being killed.'

'I didn't fetch the tip from No-Man's-Land myself,' he added, fearing that he should get the credit for something that was done by a man from the trenches.

The Nottingham City Council later decided:

That Flight-Commander Captain Albert Ball, D.S.O., M.C., being a person of distinction within the meaning of the honorary freedom of the Boroughs Act, 1885, be admitted an honorary freeman of the City of Nottingham, in recognition of the great services rendered by him as an officer of the Royal Flying Corps in connection with the operations of the British Expeditionary Force in France, and as a mark of the appreciation of his fellow-citizens of his bravery in the face of the enemy.

'Am simply dreading the Freedom affair,' wrote Ball from London, 'and really if I had myself to please I should not be within 200 miles of Nottingham on that day. However, let me know when it is and I will buck up and come.'

And so, with all the quaint ceremonial which survives in the ancient towns of Old England, Albert Ball was enrolled as a freeman of the city, on 19 February 1917.

The Mayor (Councillor Pendleton) came forward to make a stirring speech, describing the boy as 'the greatest living expert in aerial warfare'. Enclosed in a silver casket was the certificate. Ball hoped he would be a worthy successor of the honoured citizens already on the roll of freemen, and added: 'I am hoping to be out at the front again very soon. My only desire is to serve my country and my native city, of which I am justly proud.'

Ball's arrival home coincided with Zeppelin activity over England, in which, as was officially disclosed, the Midlands were not neglected.

'Let's hope the Zepps. will come to Nottingham when Ball is here,' was the sort of comment one heard in the streets.

'I shall try to join a Zepp. strafing squadron during my rest at home,' Ball had said. 'Of course,' he added, 'it'll be great sport.'

However, the authorities at home thought differently.

'I called at the War Office,' wrote Ball, on 20 October 1916, during his previous stay in England, 'and these were my orders: "On no account are you to go for a Zepp., not even if it passes just over your head. Also, you will now be used in order to teach other people to fight."'

'Home after a hundred fights' were the words on a picture placard showing a photograph of himself, his father, mother, and sister. But all this flattery and hero-worship did not spoil Ball one little bit. It amused him very much, but he could not take it very seriously. Conceit was not in his nature, and those people who enjoyed the acquaintance of Ball in those days when he was being acclaimed everywhere as a super-airman, will remember how simple and unaffected were his words and his manner.

The present writer recalls arriving at his home in Nottingham. It has already been indicated that Ball disliked talking about himself, and it was a difficult task to persuade him to talk about his fights.

It was while waiting in the hall of the house that one heard strange sounds, reminiscent of the jungle, coming from upstairs: 'That is him,' said his mother. A few seconds later, preceded by an unearthly yell, there came tumbling down the staircase a schoolboy in the uniform of an officer of the Royal Flying Corps. A short, stocky fellow, rather below the medium height, with somewhat untidy dark hair, a round jolly face, fresh complexion, and a pair of eyes brimming with laughter.

This was Captain Albert Ball. The first time he spoke he laughed. It seemed to the visitor at that time that the boy could not open his mouth without laughing. It was only when the object of the visit was explained that he pulled rather a wry face, and begged to be excused. However, his nature was much too genial to be obdurate under pressure, and once he started to talk he could not restrain his enthusiasm. It was not so much about his own work as about the science of flying and the art of fighting in the air that made him become animated.

He went to a corner of the room and produced a large object shaped like a basin, the outside painted a vivid red. This, he explained, was the nose-cap – the red spinner which he always wore on his machine as an identification mark. It was not so much, he said, to inform the Germans who it was in the machine – although they knew very well – as the familiar red mark was not adopted by anybody else in the Flying Corps. He took it with him mainly to avoid there being any doubt when he brought down an enemy machine.

'You see,' he said, 'the chaps know for certain it's me when they see this red buzzer, and whenever it is possible we must make quite certain what happened to the Hun before making a report.'

Ball, it seems, was extremely conscientious in making out his reports, and there is no doubt that he often did not do himself and his work justice. During this conversation, he said that although sometimes he had seen a machine that he had beaten going down completely out of control and in flames and he was not sure there were any witnesses, he would dive to within a few feet of the ground in order that he could see that the machine was in ruins. As most of his opponents were brought down over the enemy lines, sometimes miles in the rear, he took great risks in satisfying himself that neither the machine nor the pilot would be able to fight again.

'What is the trick that enables you to beat the Hun?' he was asked. 'Well,' he replied, 'there is no harm in telling you, because the Huns must know all about it. You see, whenever a German finds us trying a new dodge and he has a chance of getting away, he scoots off and goes back and tells his pals about it.'

Then he went on to describe his tricks of diving under the enemy machines and firing their petrol tanks.

At this time he had rather a poor opinion of the capabilities of the German pilots and said that as a rule they were disinclined to show fight except when in superior numbers. He also complained of sometimes having flown for hours over the enemy lines without being able to find an opponent.

> You often have to get up very quick [he said] to catch a Hun who will fight. Occasionally one comes alone over our lines, but by the time you get into the air he'd done a scoot. Early one morning a Hun came near the aerodrome where I was quartered. Anxious not to lose the chance, I did not waste time in dressing, but went up in my pyjamas. But I was too late. As soon as he saw my machine he was off home, and it was too cold for a long flight in pyjamas ... I have been hoping to bring a Hun down like this, but I've had no luck.

It was during this talk that Ball told of his celebrated fight with the German who was not afraid – the contest ending in a draw after each had exhausted their ammunition.

Ball seemed to have something of an affection for this Hun and often wondered who he was. Indeed, he never expressed any detestation for the German flying men, although he had seen and heard enough about the German atrocities to realize that the Germans were a race of barbarians who had not spared women and children.

His great regret was that he had not met one of the 'crack' German airmen, Immelmann, Boelcke, or Richthofen.

'They may have been in squadron fights in which I was engaged, but I could never pick them out,' he said.

Brigadier-General Higgins in his appreciation of Ball, printed at the beginning of this volume, says that one of his greatest physical qualifications as a fighting pilot was his very keen sight – he had a kind of genius for seeing German machines.

The present writer remembers being impressed at the time by Ball's eyes. They were brilliant eyes, never still and they seemed to take in everything.

During his stay in England Captain Ball went to Buckingham Palace to be decorated by the King with the DSO and two bars, and a happy family party accompanied him on that occasion. Writing previous to the event he said, 'I have been to arrange about being decorated, and it will take place soon. You will be able to come to town and spend a few days with me.'

The same week he was invited to one of Mr Lloyd George's famous breakfast parties. 'I had breakfast,' he wrote, 'with the Right Honourable Lloyd George and his daughter yesterday. It was very nice.'

It was the intention of the authorities to keep Ball at home engaged in the duties of an instructor. Before taking up this work he had a brief holiday at Skegness, but he could not rest on earth altogether, and there was something of a 'busman's holiday' about his stay there. The inhabitants of Skegness were able to see the famous Hun strafer performing various breathless evolutions in the clouds, in the course of which he looped the loop and dropped messages to acquaintances in the town.

One Sunday afternoon, Luton was enlivened by a visit from Ball, who it will be remembered, was at one time stationed there with his old regiment, the Sherwood Foresters. He first of all alighted from a one-seater. Then he came again in a two-seater and offered to take the Mayor of Luton up for a flight. The Mayor was not available at the time, so his place was taken by an Inspector of Police.

For a time Ball settled down to the work of instructing in England. It was his job to teach his methods to other men and to let them benefit as much as possible from his experience.

A group photograph taken after Albert Ball's investiture with the DSO, London, 19 November 1916. Left to right: Captain Ball's father; his sister; Ball himself; his mother.

Flying, the organ of aviation said, 'His methods were startlingly original, and we may be sure that our air service has profited by his initiative and resourcefulness.'

Brigadier-General Charlton at a later date recalled that it was said that Ball could have stayed at home and have done equally useful work in England. He was indeed urged to stay. Time after time the General had been importuned by letter and personal interview to allow Ball to return to France, although it was pointed out to the airman that he would be most usefully employed in England in training others to carry on his work in his own special way – creating duplicates of himself.

At this time Ball's younger brother Cyril was learning to fly. 'You will see me with grey hairs in my head,' he wrote to his sister. 'Oh, and the excitement we get in the air nearly sends one daft at times, but it is fine work. One practice – we have to stand upon the seat of the machine and fire at a dummy machine passing by. At times one almost falls out. I was sorry Albert didn't come back here, it would have been topping to have had him instructing us.'

The brothers were able to fly together during Albert's stay in England, and it was during one of these flights that Albert cut his lip and sustained one of the few superficial injuries that he met with while flying. At the time he said he always felt safer flying in the war zone than in England.

A good story is told of two youths who, having seen Ball fly, came up to him and said they were anxious to join the RFC and were quite willing to die for their country.

'You're no use,' laughed Ball, 'we want fellows who are anxious to live for their country, not to die.'

The airman himself got tired of living in England. The desire to get back to the front grew stronger every day until he could not resist it any longer, although he knew there were other people to think of besides himself. He told his old tutor M. Ami Bauman that he had brought down thirty-two enemy machines and that he would soon be going back to France he hoped – to try and get eight more and thus beat the record of the famous Frenchman Guneymer.

Apart from his work of instruction he had been far from idle. He had designed a fast-flying scout machine, the plans of which he gave to the British Government.

Ball was an expert in most matters connected with aeroplane construction. He knew the relative values of aeroplane engines and all about them, and about behaviour of various types of magnetic compass in an aeroplane when in flight. He concentrated more especially on the basis to be adopted in designs to secure adequate strength in high speed machines. A minimum of weight in order to secure a maximum of speed, together with innovations in the matter of sight and protection, were what he sought to embody in planning his machine. He considered he reduced the difficulties to a minimum, and there were experts who agreed with him. However, he did not live to see his design adopted by the Government.

He had ambitious plans for flying and for aeroplane construction after the war. He was repeatedly urged to seize the chance to stop in England and make the most of his opportunities. He was offered a large sum to leave flying and devote himself exclusively to the constructional side.

'Not until I have finished my job out there,' said Ball.

Before 25 February he had made up his mind. 'On Monday I go to join the 56th Squadron,' he wrote, 'and shall do all in my power to get O.K. and ready for France. I am sorry I am not going out at once, but one cannot get everything.' Three days later he said, 'Well, here I am and very nice too. General Henderson's son is here, and many other good chaps. Tons of work is done and altogether it is a good place. My flight is 'A' flight, and I mean to be ' A' in every way, also the men in it.'

When he was getting ready for France it was noted that the name on his kit bag was still '2nd Lieut. Albert Ball.' It was suggested that the word 'Captain' ought to be painted on it. 'Oh, they'll know it's mine alright,' he said.

Just before he returned to France a little girl called at his father's house and begged him to accept as a mascot a black velvet cat, to be fixed on the front of his machine. Ball took it eagerly with both hands.

Later on he wrote home to say that the mascot had brought him luck.

CHAPTER 13

Back to the Front

Writing from London on 14 November to his mother, Ball said:

Have at last finished with the War Office. Well, dear, I am feeling full of thought, and not at all in the right state for sleep. I have offered to go out again and have another smack. I don't offer, dear, because I want to go, but because every boy who has loving people and a good home should go out and stand up for it. You think I have done enough, but, oh, no, there is not or at least should not be such a thought in such a war as this. Don't think me unfair wishing to go again, for I don't do it because I wish to. I shall find it hard to go, but you will all back me up, and I will try again to help my country and bring credit to my dear mother.

It will take a short time to arrange things. I expect it may even be a month. I thought I would send you this letter, for I am feeling all poo-poo, and it always helps me if I tell my mother.

But he did not go back until some months later – 7 April – because the authorities considered that his work at home, the advice he was able to give to pilots out of his own great experiences, was of more value to the country than his services at the front.

I cannot leave dear old England [he wrote just before flying across the Channel] without a word of thanks to you. My leave has been so happy. It is hard to leave such dear people, but you are brave as well as dear and it makes it less hard.

It is an honour to be able to fight and do one's best for such a country and for such dear people. I shall fight for you and come home for you, and God always looks after me and makes me strong; may He look after you also.

It was with these words that Albert Ball went back to the front for the last time. The spirit in which he went back was the spirit of sublime self-sacrifice which he and thousands of others who might have stopped at home, have shown in this war against barbarism.

His arrival in France was a signal demonstration that it was the old Ball, as brilliant and resourceful as ever, who had come back. He flew across the Channel and, reaching our lines, made straight for a number of German aeroplanes that were circling over, apparently unaware who it was that was coming for them. There was a great fight, and as a result, Ball put two machines out of action before descending to report to Headquarters that he had arrived from England.

According to one correspondent:

His companions were together in an aerodrome waiting for the return of Captain Ball, who was flying over from England. When he landed with his machine, he gave an account of a short excursion he had made over the German lines where he had been attacked by two adversaries and sent one of them crashing to the ground.

'Why have you done that?' asked the Colonel.

'To lose no time,' was Ball's instant reply.

The only reference to this in his diary is: 'Arrived 5 p.m.'

The machine in which Ball left Britain for France for the last time.

Next page: Captain Ball leaving the aerodrome to fly across to France.

His first letter said:

Dearest People,
Oh, what a topping time we are having. No kit has left England
yet, and it will not do so until the 16th. However, I am in France,
and we shall start work in about a week, so I am very happy. I
am just sending you this line so that you will know everything is
O.K. I will write a real letter later. Cheero. I do hope you are all
O.K. Tons of love.

'Cheero,' he wrote later, 'am just about to start the great game
again. Oh, how nice it will be. I will try so hard to be a credit to
you.' And again:

Cheero, am so very happy. All my machines and officers are at last
ready for war. We hope to have a smack in a day or two. It has been
a big job getting all O.K., but now things are fine. All is perfectly
ready, so you bet I am very happy. I am taking my Flight on a test
patrol at 7 a.m. I have got another red cowl on my machine.

There had been great changes at the front during Ball's long
leave. The personnel and equipment of the Air Services had
been enormously strengthened during the winter months, and
other young pilots had been making names for themselves by
their brilliant work. Vast preparations were well advanced for
the great offensives that were launched early in the spring in
Flanders against the Hindenburg line, on the salient between
the Scarpe and the Ancre, and on the Arras side including the
Vimy Ridge.

Sir Douglas Haig's references in his dispatch to the part
played by the Air Services at the beginning of the offensive
must be quoted here because they relate to the region about
Arras where Ball performed some of the most brilliant exploits
of his career.

The great strength of these defences [says the British Commander-in-Chief] demanded very thorough artillery preparation, and they in turn could only be carried out effectively with the aid of our air services.

Our activity in the air therefore increased with the growing severity of our bombardment. A period of very heavy air fighting ensued, culminating in the days immediately preceding the attack in a struggle of the utmost intensity for local supremacy in the air. Losses on both sides were severe, but the offensive tactics most gallantly persisted in by our fighting aeroplanes secured our artillery from serious interference, and enabled our guns to carry out their work effectively.

At the same time, bombing machines caused great damage and loss to the enemy by a constant succession of successful raids directed against his dumps, railways, aerodromes and billets.

Ball, it will be seen, timed his arrival very well. He left England on 7 April. On 9 April the first great blow was struck by the Third and First armies, under the command respectively of General Allenby and General Horne.

It will be recalled that in 1916, Ball arrived in France a few days before the beginning of the first battle of the Somme. Both in 1916 and 1917 he returned to plunge into battle just when the fight was hottest and when he was most wanted. During the great battle of Arras he was flying over the German lines all day. The official reports of the RFC continually refer to the presence of his machine thereabouts. Between Arras and Lens he fought his last great fights. Again and again he attacked sometimes single-handed twelve and fourteen machines. The German airmen were fighting hard, and were not so disposed to run away as of yore, so that Ball had all the fighting he could have desired.

There were new developments in the aerial warfare at this time, low-flying aeroplanes kept in touch with the advancing infantry, sent word about the latest positions they occupied, and signalled as soon as they spotted enemy preparations for counter-attacks. They also attacked the German infantry with machine gun fire and bombs. Information of concentration of enemy troops was sent to the artillery, who dispersed them by accurate fire directed by signals from above.

The German aerodromes were attacked again and again, and the railway stations were continuously assaulted by well directed bombs.

Sir Douglas Haig subsequently paid this tribute to the work of the Royal Flying Corps:

> In the discharge of duties, constantly increasing in number and importance, the Royal Flying Corps throughout the whole of the past year has shown the same magnificent offensive spirit which characterised its work during the Somme battle, combined with unsurpassed technical knowledge and practical skill.

Ball did not figure much in this work. He was more or less of a free lance, flying as a rule at great altitudes and attacking groups of the enemy machines. Large numbers of these enemy machines were concentrated on this Arras front when Ball arrived.

Our advance was hindered by bad weather with heavy falls of snow and squalls of wind and rain, which delayed the bringing up of reinforcements, and gave the enemy more time to organise counter-attacks. But the bad weather did not stop our flying men altogether. The German Army was fighting desperately to resist the slow but certain advance of our men, and the British airmen were able to give their comrades most valuable aid.

But Ball was not quite satisfied, and seemed rather anxious about the machine he had, judging by the following letter: 'They have put me on a machine, but I should like to get back to my old machine as soon as possible; oh, I shall never be able to do my job. I must fly another machine and then I shall get along with the job.'

Two days later all was O.K., as he would have said: 'I had tea at the General's house to-day. He has decided to give me the machines I wanted.'

His wish gratified, Ball was perfectly happy, and the Huns soon knew that he was back again. The red cowl was the danger signal which they knew only too well, and the German airmen probably were aware that he was about very soon after his re-appearance.

'Oh, what a topping day it has been,' he wrote to his fiancé on 14 April. 'First of all I had my first two flights this morning. In the first one the Hun ran off, but in the second I managed to get a few rounds in and made him run. In a few days we shall start real work, and then I hope to have tons of sport.'

But the next day he was rather down in the mouth, for there had been heavy casualties. It was a day on which the enemy counterattacked with large forces, and there was corresponding activity in the air.

> ... Am feeling very poo-poo today [he wrote]. Five of my best pals were done in yesterday, and I think it is so rotten.
>
> We have not got our machines ready yet, but when we do, oh, I do hope we shall let them have it.
>
> I had my two flight yesterday, but the C.O. will not let me have my prop, until all the machines are ready. I do so want to get at them, but I suppose they know best.

Soon news began to come through to his native city of new triumphs.

Said one account,

> Graphic details of aerial combats in which Captain Ball distinguished himself are told by a comrade of the R.F.C.

Immediately Ball returned to the front, he was posted with us for risky duty behind the German line, or in advance of our own army. For the first fortnight he was absolutely tireless. He was up every day. It was in that period he brought down the most of the twelve enemy machines he added to his bag, which then totalled about 30 more or less, probably more.

Without doubt he is the bravest and boldest lad who ever wore wings. In the recent period of severe fighting he made his mark on the enemy as well as among us. As soon as he appeared to attack a prospective victim the German generally made off. Only once lately did I see the enemy put up a real fight against him. As we retired from a raid, the Germans suddenly appeared to cut us off. Ball dashed at two of the enemy machines, the finest of their kind on the Western Front, actually driving his own machine between the two. For a time the three machines twisted and wriggled and squirmed. Ball got in first. One German machine reeled and went down like a winged bird. The second German was trying hard to get Ball while he was finishing off the first. He made a swoop to catch the Nottingham lad at a disadvantage, but the latter swerved clear and instead of being the victim, brought down his man.

By the end of the first week, he had accounted for five enemy machines.

Here is an account of his life during those first days of April gathered from a French source.

Ball attacks two Albatross in two places, one of which went towards the east, whilst the other, damaged, crashed to the ground. A little later Ball discovered five Albatrosses above Cambrai. He goes close, fires point blank, the machine falls, the other four flee.

The second day Ball patrolled at 4,000 metres, and observed an enemy squadron quitting the aerodrome. He sets out for the

165

fray when the machines are 2,000 metres up. He starts on the first and machine guns it at 20 metres, and the Bosche falls. At this moment Ball notices that he is separated from his lines by the enemy formation. He tries to force a passage, fails, then he flies towards the south-east followed by the enemy machines. Ball waits until his enemies swarm together then he turns, swoops down in amongst them, and can at last return to his own lines.

The third day he starts by forcing a Bosche to come down to earth, then he attacks and destroys the Albatross. He had posted himself in the clouds waiting. An Albatross appears, Ball pursues it, the adversary descends towards the earth, Ball follows at 200 metres. His machine is attacked by another aeroplane, the controls are broken with the exception of one, the side is damaged, the machine wobbles. Ball is lost! But no! He re-establishes the equilibrium, returns to the aerodrome and makes a marvellous landing.

Within a period of two weeks of his reappearance in France, he had accounted for another ten aeroplanes.

Several extracts from his diary follow together with various letters. The weather was evidently not to his liking.

Says his diary on 21 April: 'Dud day. So flew to—. Flew over lines at night. Had scrap, with two Albatross scouts, fired 1½ drums but only cleared them off.'

On 23 April he wrote home:

Dearest People,

Am so fagged to-night, but feel that I must send you a line. We did our first two real jobs today, and I got two Huns—one I crashed, and the other I set on fire. I had six fights altogether. One of the Huns I got with a Nieuport, and one with a S.E. My machines were very badly hit about, and are having new planes to-night. Well, now I am on a job at 5 a.m., so simply must sleep.

Writing on the same day to his fiancé about these same fights, he said:

> I had three fights, and managed to bring one down, crashed in a road. This I did with my Nieuport.
>
> After coming down I had to have five new planes, for the Hun had got about fifteen shots through my spars.
>
> Well, next I went up in my S.E. 5, and had a very poo-poo time – five shots in my right strut, four in the planes, and two just behind my head. This was done by five Albatross Scouts, but I got one of them and set it on fire at 14,000 ft.
>
> Poor old chap inside. I should simply hate to be set on fire. The G—l rang up and congratulated me, also the C.O. of our wing.

The 'poor old chap,' as Ball called the German, might have been a little consoled had he known of the regrets of his chivalrous foe.

The next message was written on the back of a photo group on 25 April, time 11 p.m.:

> Dearest People,
> This photo was taken just before leaving England. I have marked a cross at the right side of the heads of our chaps. A few of the chaps in other Flights were away. Have got four Huns in my Flight to-day, and I got two of these myself. One other Hun has been got by a chap in another Flight. I am on patrol at 5 a.m. tomorrow.

Ball must have realised that he was the special mark of the entire German Air Service, but the knowledge scarcely alarmed him. He continued to go on in the same way, often flying for hours quite alone miles behind the German lines.

These entries in his diary need no explanation.

A group shot of RFC pilots. Captain Ball is seated in the front row, second from right. Ball describes the men marked with crosses as 'our chaps'.

His diary says, 23 April: 'Went on patrol. Had two combats with one, then two Albatrosses. Crashed one. General congrats.' 24 April: 'Attacked Albatross but had gun trouble.' 26 April: 'Dud day. Went on patrol, saw nothing. At night cleared up, so went out and attacked 20 Huns. I got two of them at Cambrai. Arrived back at dark with all ammunition used up.'

We know very little more about this fight of one against twenty, and we can only try and imagine this boy and his machine surrounded by a host of enemies, accepting their challenge and trying to fight his way through single-handed.

He said something about the encounter in a letter to his fiancé the next day:

> I was attacked by twenty last night and had to fire all my ammunition, getting two of them. It was dark when I returned, and everyone thought that I must have been done in, but I had to stop on their side until it was dark, for I could not fight my way through without ammunition. My right plane was hit a few times, and I had to have a new one.

According to his diary, the twenty Huns were met in four successive groups of five each. 'Attacked four lots of Huns with five in each group,' he says. 'Brought down two and able to get back without any ammunition when dark.'

In the same letter he sent the news that he had brought his total to thirty-four, and that he was trying hard to beat the record of his French rival.

But the Huns were elusive, and tried to find safety in numbers – a resource which failed against Ball.

> I have now got another two Huns [he said] making four this time, and my total is thirty-four. Only three more to be got before I am top of England and France again. In order to whack the German man [Boelcke], I'd love to get about ten more. If it's God's will that I should do it, then I will come home; oh, I do so hope it can be managed ...
>
> To-night if it clears up I am taking all my Flight out for a real good smack ... for I am off on my Nieuport then, and at 5.30 I come back and do a job on S.E. 5 with my Flight. You see they do one or two jobs each day, and I lead them, but during the remainder of the day I go up in my Nieuport and have a try myself. This is the only way to get them. Just keep at them all day.

It was Ball's instinct of sportsmanship that made him want to get ten more. He got them, but he never came home.

Ball often went out like this on his own account, and little was seen of him sometimes until it was dark when he would come planing down in time for dinner. He once spoke of the tragedy and comedy of those evening meals. The places at the table in the Mess were always set for the number of officers who were there in the afternoon. Towards the evening they returned in ones and twos and threes. It would get late and perhaps there was still two or three vacant places at the table.

'Where is —?' and 'Has — come back yet?' were enquiries that were made. Sometimes they did come back and all the places were taken, and all was merry.

But sometimes the men did not return, the vacant places were never filled, and it was a quiet restrained dinner-party.

Evening after evening when it was quite dark, Ball's place at the table was empty, but there was never any anxiety about him. Presently the hum of his engine would be heard and in a few minutes the airman would turn in, looking very tired but all smiles.

Towards the end of April, to use his favourite expression, he was not exactly 'O.K.'. He lost one of the men in his Flight, and all the controls of his own machine were shot away.

> ... I have now made my total 35. Last night I went out on patrol with my Flight and had four fights, but in the end one of my chaps was brought down crashed, and I had all my controls shot away, but I got back and am still going strong.
>
> G. Trenchard came to see me to-day, and congratulated me. He asked me if I would like two weeks in England, but I think I had better stay until all is O.K. and the month up.
>
> I am spending two days with the French R.F.C., and then my new machine will be ready, I hope. Oh, I do wish I had it ready now, for I do hate waiting.

On 28 April his diary says: 'Got up at 5.30. Dud day, so worked in garden. Got garden ready to set peas. Went on patrol at night. Attacked four Huns, brought one down. Had my control shot away, but got home O.K. General came and congratulated me.'

On some days flying was almost impossible owing to the low clouds and drizzling rain. But our airmen were tireless, and whenever there was any possibility of flying they would go up and at a low altitude bomb hostile munition dumps, railway stations, and aerodromes, besides attacking with machine gun fire parties of German infantry. There was strong opposition from the enemy fighting machines at times, and a very large number of combats took place at low altitudes with heavy casualties on both sides, many damaged machines crashing when flying near the ground, there being no chance to regain control.

According to one letter honours were easy after four fights on 28 April:

Went out with my four officers, had four fights, and got one Hun. One of my chaps brought down, crashed, and in the end all my control was shot away when I got back. General Trenchard came to-day and congratulated me. Please send me at once a box of ammunition for my automatic. Simply must close for I am so fagged.

P.S. – Total Huns now 35. Two more to beat the Frenchman.

The pursuit after the Frenchman's record was now getting very hot, and Ball was straining every nerve to add to his total. He came back night after night thoroughly exhausted after many hours spent in the air chasing Huns, some of whom refused to fight. His machines were getting badly knocked about. He was, however, by no means pleased with himself, and was quite frank about it in a letter to his fiancé:

May 3rd.

... I have been having such a poo-poo time. I will just tell you what has been taking place, you will then understand.

Firstly, a few days ago my first S.E. 5 had all its controls shot away, and that had to be sent to the doctor. I got the Hun that sent me down first, also I managed to land without crashing. Well, I got a new S.E. 5, and all went well for a day or two, but then my gun gear went wrong, and I am now at the doctor's with it.

You don't know what a beastly game it is when nothing is going as it should, and you have not got enough men to do the jobs. Last night I came off my patrol, got two Huns, and was feeling very pleased with life.

The Squadron gave a concert at night and I went. Everyone was very pleased, for I am now one in front of the Frenchman. My total is 38.

All went well until about 10 p.m. when the fire-bell went. I rushed out, and oh, try to picture how pleased I was when I saw my hut, greenhouse, and bathroom on fire. Well, I nearly had a double fit. I had taken so much trouble in getting it nice, so that when I came in at night I could have a few hours' real rest.

The G—l is giving me two S.E. 5's, so I shall then be O.K.

The same note of disappointment was evident in the message he sent home on the same day to his parents. The trouble with his machines worried him, although he was adding to his total every day and doing as well as ever he did in the course of his career, and had actually beaten the record of his French rival by 3 May. On the evening of 2 May a fire did considerable damage to his hut:

May 3rd.

Dearest People,

Am so sorry that I am not sending you all the letters that you so well deserve, but my dear people, it is quite impossible, but I am doing all I can.

My total up to last night was 38. I got two last night. Oh, it was a topping fight. About 20 of the Huns and 15 of ours. Well, now I will tell you just why I don't get the chance to write. First of all, a few days ago all my controls were shot away on my S.E.'s, but I got the Hun that did it. That machine had to go to the doctor; it is still there, but it will be finished soon. Secondly, I got a new S.E., but it is now out of order and I am now at the doctor's with it. It is all trouble, and it is getting on my mind. Am feeling very old just now. Well, to top the lot, last night the Squadron gave a concert and all were very pleased, for I am now one in front of the Frenchman. All went well until 10 p.m., when the fire-bell rang. I rushed out. Oh, try to picture my delight when I saw my hut, greenhouse, and bathroom all on fire. Well, I had a double fit, but that did not put the fire out. But I ask you, how can I write letters under such conditions? I am just writing this in my spare moment at A.D., so do excuse it. I just felt that I must drop you a line before another day went. Will try to get O.K. soon, and then will write tons. Cheero, am off on another patrol in an hour's time. Tons of love.

As soon as the weather improved, Ball and his men were everywhere making their presence felt. He attacked the Germans on sight whatever their strength was, and his example was a great spur to his comrades. The German losses were very heavy, probably heavier than was officially reported in our communique. We know, for instance, that Ball himself never claimed a victim until he was absolutely certain about it; but, of course, it was not always possible to get confirmation. According to one report he met a squadron of Hun planes and picked out his first opponent, who immediately descended followed by Ball, while the rest of the hostile squadron swiftly manoeuvred to place themselves between Ball and the British lines. Without hesitation he dashed for the lot of them. Five remained in their previous formation, and two Albatrosses advanced to meet him. He out-manoeuvred the vanguard and afterwards succeeded in shooting the pair down. Somehow he outwitted the other five and arrived home in triumph with two more victims to his credit.

There is the story of two Albatrosses who made direct for him, and then one evidently recognising who he was quickly retired. The second one turned to do the same, but was too late and fell in flames.

Describing his visits to the front a Spanish correspondent gave these impressions of Ball:

> The last day of our visit two Captains of the R.F.C. arrived. One of them was still a boy, short, unkempt, with staring eyes, and shy looking.
>
> 'Captain Ball,' said the officer in charge of the introductions.
>
> Captain Ball, like so many of his compatriots, was unable to put much eloquence into his conversation; he spoke of his bag of forty-two as if he was half ashamed of having destroyed them! But his colleagues in the Service spoke of him with emulation and pride.
>
> Captain Ball was a sportsman in the blood, and oblivious of the danger to himself – two good qualities which are 'ideals' amongst the British people. Captain Ball was the man who on ten occasions had risked his life to save the life of another aviator. Ball was the man who, after having destroyed two German aeroplanes, arrived at the aerodrome, gave the message, took his provision of petrol, and a few minutes after was flying over the enemy lines and returned an hour later to announce that he had destroyed another two enemy machines.

Captain Ball in the cockpit of his aircraft.

CHAPTER 14

Triumph

Perhaps the most striking and crushing victory of Ball's career was on the occasion when quite alone he was suddenly attacked by five enemy machines. Flying away did not seem to him the best way of dealing with the situation; he determined to make the best of a desperate position by fighting. He started off by destroying two enemy machines, and then he let himself fall almost vertically, doing what airmen call the 'death-leap.' Ten yards from the ground he stopped his fall. One of the three remaining Germans failing to manoeuvre his machine with the expert precision of the Britisher, went crashing to the earth. Before the other two were able to get into favourable positions, Ball had soared above, and quickly destroyed one of them. The last one of the five, terrified by what he had seen, hurried away and managed to escape. Ball had thus accounted for four enemy machines in less than ten minutes.

At the beginning of May, he was bringing down German machines regularly at the rate of nearly two a day.

This was about the time that the final British attacks in the Arras offensive were taking place. A great breach had been made in the Hindenburg line and we had taken some 20,000 prisoners and captured something like 60 square miles of territory. In this great success our airmen had had a big share, and it was over this part of the country that Ball was bringing down the enemy machines.

The neighbourhood of Arras, Lens, Douai and Cambrai where he was operating must have been a zone of ill-fame to the German airmen.

There was no doubt that ever since Ball's return to action the Germans had been laying all manner of traps to catch him. On almost every occasion he and his comrades met a German squadron the British boys were outnumbered, and he does not mention one single occasion when he fought alone on equal terms.

In these last days it seems no German airman was prepared to face Ball alone in the air and fight it out, although the German champions would have had very little difficulty in finding him if they had so desired.

There was no mistaking the British machine with the red cowl. But it was not the tactics of the enemy to risk the lives of their best flyers in an equal fight with the boy. Their plan was to fall upon him and break him by sheer weight of numbers.

His diary for the first two days of May shows how hard he was hitting the enemy: 'May 1st. Went a patrol at night. Attacked two lots of Huns. Crashed one, forced down another. Returned at 8.30.

'May 2nd. Went on patrol at 6 p.m. Had four combats. Crashed two Huns.'

On 3 May he had a rare encounter with a pair of Albatross scouts. They were good fighters, and put up a strong opposition. After a prolonged struggle he managed to hit both of them, but nearly lost his own life. One Albatross, after being struck, made a desperate attempt to ram the British machine. The German had evidently made up his mind that he was going under and was determined to bring Ball down with him. His machine only missed colliding by inches. Then the German was shot down, and Ball turned and quickly out-manoeuvring the second machine, put it out of action also. After that he was compelled to go down, for his own machine was considerably damaged.

The impressions of a Portuguese visitor to the British Front are worth recording. He spoke of Ball as

> Adored by his squadron ... a magnificent example to his subordinates. At all times, immediately he perceived an enemy, he fell upon him as an eagle on its prey. Only complete squadrons dared to attack him, but he darted into the middle, frightening them by the terrible precision of his machine-guns. He would descend upon an adversary, fly from one to another with such courage and science that the Boches sought refuge in flight at full speed.

The Portuguese gentleman gave a descriptive account of the fight already mentioned:

> In one of his last combats which he fought against two Fokkers, one of the German aviators mad with rage upon seeing the machine of his comrade out of the combat, darted all at once upon Ball in a fit of desperation, thinking by colliding his machine with that of his adversary he would kill himself but would also destroy the English 'ace.' With a rapid glance Ball divined the intentions of his opponent, and with a risky turn freed himself. Flying immediately at his enemy he drove him down with his machine-gun.

One of his comrades who was often with him at this time when Ball was strewing the ground with the wrecks of his opponents, has pointed out that Ball had scarcely time to put in any reports, about these fights. 'It's one thing to bring enemy machines down, and quite another to write all about it,' said this comrade, 'and you know poor old Ball had had so many combat reports within the past few days that he had had hardly time to look over his 'plane at all.'

Ball, it is said, was to have been made a Major, but the prospect of restricted opportunities for crossing the enemy lines made him resist promotion with a respectful persistence.

On the two days previous to his last battle, Ball had some thrilling fights, bringing down three machines and putting many others to flight. Mr Percival Phillips has thus described them:

On May 5th, while patrolling, he sighted two hostile craft, and as he was fairly low he flew away from them, climbing steadily. When the German aeroplanes were quite near his tail, Captain Ball swerved sharply, slid underneath one of his opponents, 'and turned on his machine-gun. The German fell out of control.

Captain Ball then manoeuvred in order to attack the second enemy machine, but it flew straight at him, firing steadily. Captain Ball returned the fire as the German came full tilt at him, and a collision seemed inevitable, when the hostile machine suddenly went down. The engine of Captain Ball's machine was hit, and the pilot drenched with oil.

No other hostile aircraft were in sight, so Captain Ball dropped and saw both German aeroplanes lying completely wrecked within four hundred yards of each other. As he came home he fell in with two other hostile aircraft, but as his ammunition was exhausted and his sights covered with oil, he reluctantly 'put his nose down' and returned to the aerodrome.

Next day Captain Ball was out as usual roving the sky for battle, when – at a height of something over two miles – he came on four red Albatross scouts of a new type. He dived straight into the centre of the formation, and broke it up, then slipped under the nearest machine, firing his machine-gun until it dropped out of control. That was sufficient for the three surviving Albatrosses. They turned tail and broke off the fight.

His diary says: 'May 5th. Went up, but saw nothing. Went on patrol at night. Had combat with two Albatross scouts. Got them down-crashed but was myself hit in engine. Am four ahead of Frenchman [Guynemer].' It was on 5 May that he wrote his last letter to his fiancé telling of his triumphs but also hoping for the day when there would be no more killing. As we know he often longed for that day. He wanted the 'great sport' without the killing.

He begins this letter with a word about his garden:

May 5th, 1917.

… You see my garden always causes a lot of sport, and when I am happy I dig in the garden and sing. I don't get much time off, but what I get is enjoyed.

Well, I made my total 40 last night, and G. Trenchard rang up to say I am going to be presented to G. Sir D. H. To-morrow. I am very pleased and know you will be. Oh, won't it be nice when all this beastly killing is over, and we can just enjoy ourselves and not hurt anyone. I hate this game, but it is the only thing one must do just now.

I went up on patrol at 5 p.m. and met two Albatross Scouts. I attacked the nearest and got underneath it, putting three drums of Lewis into it. The pilot was killed, and the machine crashed.

I was getting ready for the second when all at once it came for me, head on. We opened fire at the same time and made straight for each other.

Well, Bobs, I thought all was up with us, and it was going to be a ramming job. But just as we were going to hit, my engine was hit by a bullet and all the oil came into my face. For a short time I saw nothing, but when all got O.K. again, I looked down and saw the Hun going down out of control. He crashed about 400 yards from his pal.

I was again attacked on the way back, but all my ammunition was used, and I only just got back before my engine gave out.

This makes my 42nd, and the Major is very pleased.

Re hut and garden. Well, I have got it nearly right again now; in fact, I have just been lighting the petrol stove in my bath tank so that I may have a bath. It is great sport having to heat your own water before you can have a bath, but it takes about two hours to get the water.

> When I am happy I dig in the garden and sing.

Only a sensitive nature could write like that, and yet the previous night he had killed his fortieth German. And he hated the game. He did not want to go on with it. Why hurt anyone? But one must do it. It had to be done.

Many young Englishmen have gone to war thinking this. Rupert Brooke, Francis Ledwidge, and a host of other fine spirits who have perished – hated the game. But there was no other way out. They loved beauty and liberty and freedom too much to stand aside and see them destroyed.

This is the last entry in his diary: 'May 6th. Gardened in the morning. Patrolled at night. Combat with four Hun Albatross scouts. Crashed one of them down.'

And so on the last day the boy was thinking of his garden as well as of the fighting. On this day he had landed in an aerodrome on the Somme to replenish his petrol supply and have repairs done to his machine which had been badly knocked about by enemy bullets. 'All we men of the R.N.A.S. admired him so much,' said a Service man in relating the incident. Ball was photographed on this day, and a reproduction is given on another page.

The plane is patched in several places, and it will be noticed that the strut on the right-hand side has been bound up where it had been splintered by a bullet. At the top of the cockpit, just behind Captain Ball's neck a few inches away, is the mark of another bullet.

One of his last letters written to a friend in London breathes his wonderful enthusiasm:

> You will be pleased to hear that I have got ten more Huns, and my total is now forty – two in front of my French rival. Oh, I'm having a topping time. To-day or to-morrow I'm being presented to Sir Douglas Haig. Am very pleased.
>
> I just want to get a few more Huns if I can.

There is a sad, almost fatalistic note in the following letter, an extract from which is quoted at the beginning of this volume:

May 5th, 11.30 p.m.

Dearest Dad,

Cheero. Have just come in off patrol, and have made my total forty-two.

I attacked two Albatross scouts and crashed them, killing the pilots. In the end I was brought down, but am quite O.K. Oh, it was a good fight, and the Huns were fine sports. One tried to ram me, after he was hit, and only missed by inches. Am indeed looked after by God, but oh! I do get tired of always living to kill, and am really beginning to feel like a murderer. Shall be so pleased when I have finished.

Captain Ball outside his hut in France.

Have got my hut, garden, greenhouse and bath-room O.K. again now; in fact, have just been lighting the fire to heat my boiler. Shall have a fine bath soon.

General Trenchard rang up to-day in order to tell me that I am going to be presented to General Sir D. H. Am very pleased.

Don't work too hard, dad. For it will be so rotten when I come home if you cannot share my happiness.

Well, now for bath and a bed. Cheero, dear dad. Please give my dear mother a huge cheero for me, and tell her I am doing my best for her. Tons of love.

Albert.

P.S. – Do send me a few plants for my garden and greenhouse. Thanks so much for the chocs.

His last letter was written on 6 May to his sister. It was the day of his last flight:

Dearest Lol,

Received your topping letter and cake. It is so good of you to think of me so much.

To-day we drew lots for leave, and I came last, but, Lol, it was a sporting chance ...

Well, I made my forty-second Hun yesterday, so am now four in front of the French.

I am going to be presented to General Sir D. H. It will be very nice.

Was shot down yesterday, so am getting a new machine to-day.

Must close now,

Tons of love,

Albert.

The same day he flew again to fight his country's enemies, and he never came back.

CHAPTER 15

The Last Flight

There was a great mystery about the disappearance of Ball, and the official and unofficial messages threw very little light upon it. The anxious public were given a picture of Ball alone over the enemy lines flying well but cut off from his comrades and surrounded by a company of some of the best German airmen determined to make sure of their victim this time. A hot fire was coming from the guns below, and from above and all sides the machine guns of the enemy airmen were pouring shot into the British machine. There the picture faded and his friends were left to guess what happened to the brave boy. We knew that he had been similarly cut off before and had managed to wriggle out safely. Was it all really over this time? The accounts sent by the war correspondents agreed on most points.

That sent to *The Times* gave what facts were known of his last flight:

On the evening of May 7th he had gone out in company with another machine, flown by a pilot whom we will call ' M.' They met an enemy machine, which they attacked and drove down, riddled with bullets. Then a party of four Germans hove in sight, with whom the British fliers promptly closed. M. found one enemy machine in such a favourable position that he was practically at its mercy, so he put his own machine into a spin and began to go down. It must be an unpleasant experience, but it was successful in shaking off the enemy.

M. regained control of his machine, climbed up again, and re-entered the fight. He tackled one of the Germans, and after a long fight, sent it down crashing to earth. Then he turned to engage another machine, but on closing with it a bullet broke his wrist, and another carried away the top of his control lever. Thus crippled he could fight no more, but though in great pain and unable to control his machine, he managed to get over the lines and land his aeroplane undamaged in our own territory. Then he fainted.

What happened after M. was obliged to leave the field of battle is a mystery. Captain Ball was then left with three enemy machines to fight. Such odds were nothing new in Captain Ball's experience.

Another account of how Ball met his death was given by Mr Percival Phillips, of *The Daily Express*. He said:

The last aerial battle in which Captain Albert Ball took part before he was reported missing, was fought on the evening of May 7th. Captain Ball went out with a patrol squadron which encountered a German machine and riddled it with bullets, driving it down.

Four red Albatross machines then came up, and a brother-officer of Captain Ball, who may be called 'Captain X.,' engaged one of them at close range. The German manoeuvred for a favourable position, and his opponent dived and shook him off. Climbing again, Captain X. pursued another of the red enemy squadron, and fought it for a considerable time, the German machine being out-manoeuvred and sent crashing to earth. Then Captain X. engaged a third machine, but he was shot through the wrist and the top of his control-lever was carried away. Although suffering great pain, and further handicapped by the damage to his aeroplane, he succeeded in landing in the

British lines without further injury, and then fainted. There are no details as to what happened to Captain Ball.

Captain X., who is a South African, hailing from Springfontein, is a brother officer of 25 years, and when in hospital, related his experience to the *Sunday Herald*:

We were up from 9,000 feet to 10,000 feet, and I managed to get over our lines. What happened to Ball I can't say. All I know is, we went up, the three of us, in bad weather, to try and get hold of the circus [our airmen's description of the Huns' team of star performers], and we all got split up. Later on, when the weather had cleared, we had lost each other. I had only been up with Ball a few times, and I hoped he was alright. He was absolutely marvellous. Anyone else would have been killed a hundred times doing what he did.

Captain Meintjes, another comrade, gave his story in *Reynold's Newspaper*:

We ascended at half-past five, and after flying together for a few miles, separated to meet again later at an appointed spot above somewhere near Cambrai, thence to proceed to Arras. Had we only decided upon Arras first and Cambrai next, Ball would probably be alive to-day, but fate decided otherwise. As it was, we ran into bad weather just after we met, and while we were more or less hidden from each other in a heavy bank of clouds, four enemy machines swooped on us from above. Four to three does not sound big odds when a man like Ball was engaged, but not only were they on top of us, but almost immediately they were reinforced by six more machines. We had been up two hours before we ran into the enemy, but the next two minutes seemed a lifetime, for the most part I was busy ridding myself of one Hun, and just as he toppled I set about looking for Ball and my other companion. Something swooped from the cloud behind me, and exactly what happened after then until I found myself pulling up just inside the lines, I will never clearly remember.

Since I have been lying here in hospital, I have often gone over the whole business in my mind, trying to fathom just what happened to dear old Ball. They say he came down near Lille. So it must have been a head wound that finished him. Knowing the spot where the scrap occurred, I am positive he must have been blinded. Otherwise, severely wounded though he must have been, Ball would have found a better landing than Lille.

Another officer in the Royal Flying Corps gives his version of the last great struggle as follows:

The fight in which he was brought down was one of the severest I have been in. The enemy realised how much depended on their ability to keep our machines from passing over their lines. They made desperate efforts to keep us away. I had Ball under observation from the start. My impression is that the enemy had marked him down too, for immediately we approached half-a-dozen of the enemy's best fighting machines were detached from the main squadron, and went at Ball all they knew. I managed to attract two of them in my direction. That left four, and they began peppering Ball with their machine guns. He went straight at them with that fearless dash for which he is famed. He brought down one. I believe he also damaged two others so severely that they had to go down. By then the fight was raging fiercely, and for a time I lost sight of Ball.

When next I caught sight of him he appeared to be flying well over the enemy lines, and was attracting towards himself the whole efforts of the enemy. From below gunfire was coming. From above bombs were being dropped, and on either side machine guns were spitting death at him. A cloud of German machines were circling about, pecking at him just like great hawks after their prey. Ball was fighting gamely, though he appeared to be entirely cut off from our squadron by now. Some of our chaps tried to get to his assistance, but apparently the Germans realised the value of the bird they had in the toils, for a dozen of their machines were detached to engage us while the others were giving the coup de grace to Ball.

Our men had to give up. From that moment Ball disappeared in the midst of a cloud of German machines. All was a hopeless tangle. For a time it was impossible to distinguish friend from foe. The tangle was undone, and we were able to distinguish Ball's machine as it manoeuvred and fought against the great odds now against him. Gradually he became little more than a speck. Then there was a puff and a flash and the speck started down to earth. From our distance it was impossible to say exactly how he was forced down.

An account, dated 12 May, from British Headquarters in France, which reached England via the United States, said: 'He was last seen near Lens, between 6.30 and 7 p.m. At that time he was engaged with three German machines. He was not seen to fall, however.'

A communiqué from the Havas agency reported: 'It is known that he started on an expedition on the 7th May, with several of his comrades, and that he managed in the course of an engagement to bring down his forty-fourth German machine, while the two pilots who were navigating with him, were wounded and forced to come down. Ball has not turned up since.'

The impression at the time he was reported missing was that, surrounded by enemy machines, cut off from his comrades, Ball had been forced to land on enemy territory, but there was a strong hope that like so many other of his comrades, who have been brought down, he was still alive and a prisoner of war.

For many days that happy belief was held by his comrades, by his devoted family, and by the whole nation who had heard of his disappearance with the greatest anxiety, but who could not believe that this boy who had escaped death so many times and had triumphed over his foes when time after time it seemed that he was trapped, was no more.

Opposite page: The last photograph of Captain Ball.

CHAPTER 16

Missing

The following is a copy of a telegram from Major-General Trenchard, who was then commanding the Royal Flying Corps in the field, dated 8 May 1917:

> To Officer Commanding, No. 56 Squadron,
> Royal Flying Corps,
> In the Field.
>
> Am very sorry to hear that Captain Ball is missing, and I hope he may have landed safely. He was one of the most daring, skilful and successful pilots the Flying Corps has ever had. His loss will be felt by the squadron, and the whole Flying Corps.

On the same day the general wrote to Captain Ball's father:

> I very much regret having to tell you that your son, Captain Ball, is missing, but sincerely hope that he has landed safely. As you know, he was the most daring, skilful and successful pilot the Royal Flying Corps has ever had. Everybody in the Flying Corps looked upon him as their own personal asset, and he was a most popular officer. His good spirit was infectious, as whichever squadron he was with the officers of it tried to work up to his level and reputation. I have never met a man who had been so successful as he was in such a short time, so modest and so reliable.

Again sympathising with you in your loss. If we hear any more news I will see that all information is sent to you.

'It is with the very greatest regret,' wrote Major R. G. Bloomfield, his squadron commander,

that I have to inform you that your son, Captain A. Ball, is missing. Captain Ball went out on patrol with ten other pilots of this squadron on the evening of May 7th, and was very actively engaged with his usual success until 8 p.m., when he was seen not very far over the lines and perfectly all right. The light was then failing, and Captain Ball has not been seen or heard of since. It is impossible to put into words the sense of loss which I myself and the whole squadron feel. You have my deepest and most sincere sympathy.

And so for a little while nobody could or would believe that Ball's life was wholly ended. This boy, who had come back time after time with his machine perforated with holes and all but falling to pieces, who had in all weathers, at early morning, late at night, always managed to return home – it was incredible that all was over with him. Even if he was badly wounded, so long as he was conscious and capable of exercising any control over his machine, his comrades felt certain that he would have come home. It was hard to believe that he had been killed outright by a chance shot after having escaped hundreds of times. No, it must be that with his machine hopelessly crippled, he had been forced down behind the German trenches, and was now an honoured prisoner of war.

But there were grave doubts when the German wireless sent out a report: 'On May 7th two English aeroplanes were destroyed by German aviators. Lieut. Richthofen shot down an English three-decker which was piloted by Captain Ball.' About the same time, the Wolff agency circulated the following:

Our airmen were yesterday on the Western front again fighting successfully. Indeed the enemy airmen, on account of their continuous heavy losses, held back more on the whole than they have done for several days. On the Aisne front, the French sent strong squadrons against low-flying infantry observation machines, a sign of how troublesome our airmen's bold attacks and observation activities have become for the foe. The enemy lost twenty-one flying machines, four of them crashing to the earth ... Richthofen's twentieth air victim was an English fighting scout. This fighting scout is the newest English solo fighting machine, and appeared only a few weeks ago on the front, but has already fallen a sacrifice to our airmen. The pilot of the fighting scout was Captain Ball, who, according to all appearances, is the Captain Ball who, according to the announcement of the English, is supposed to have shot down thirty machines. The squadron of the commander von Richthofen conquered both the best known English fliers, first Captain Robinson, now Captain Ball, in air fighting.

Still, in spite of these definite claims by the enemy, there was no certainty that Ball was dead. It was remembered by his friends that Captain Robinson, the Zeppelin strafer, who was reported as missing very shortly after he went to the Western front, was not heard of for many days, and then the news came that he was safe and a prisoner of war. That was the great hope felt about Ball.

The Havas Agency said: 'Albert Ball, the star of aviators, who bore the anonymous glory of the British aviation, has been missing since the 7th May. Is he a prisoner or has he been killed? If he is dead, he died fighting for his forty-fifth victory.'

All the French newspapers published references: 'England's most famous airman, at the age of twenty'; 'The celebrated aviator – he whom the English call the marvel of their fifth army'; 'The super-airman, Captain Ball'; etc.

His portrait in the newspapers was conspicuous along the boulevards, together with the pictures of the propeller of one of his favourite machines and the famous red nose-cap.

Our Allies joined in the hope that the news would soon come that Ball was safe. It was pointed out that of the airmen who were brought down over the German lines, at least half escaped with their lives.

From all over the world came messages to his home and to the War Office, earnestly expressing the hope that the boy was all right. In the United States, in Canada, in South America, the millions who had heard of Ball's exploits learnt that his career was at an end, but that he was probably a prisoner of war. In Nottingham there was the very greatest public interest and anxiety.

'Is our hero safe?' asked the Nottingham papers. 'Captain Ball was so thrillingly intrepid and venturesome in his aerial flights that the risk of personal danger was always present, and the whole city ardently hopes that nothing worse may have befallen him than capture by the enemy, though that, in all conscience, is indeed an unenviable fate for anyone to have to suffer.'

Suddenly there came a burst of sunshine: 'The news that Captain Albert Ball, D.S.O., M.C., is alive and well, though a prisoner of war in Germany, will delight all who have heard tales of his amazing achievements as an air fighter,' wrote a correspondent of the *Morning Post*. '*Ball est prisonnier*' and '*Ball n'est pas mort*' were headlines in the French Press, expressing the joy of the French people. Other journals gave some detailed information: 'The Secretary of State for War has informed Captain Ball's family, who have not heard any news since May 1st of the missing airman, that he is a prisoner in Germany.' The news spread all over the world that he was safe.

An officer who actually saw him fall said: 'We are of opinion that he got down unhurt. I expect some of the German flying men will let us know later what happened, because there is a good deal of kindly feeling and admiration for each other among the two services.'

A little later, another flying officer, just returned from France, gave the information that a German airman dropped a note in the British lines stating that Captain Ball was slightly wounded but all right, and a prisoner of war.

Then a chaplain attached to the Royal Flying Corps sent this message to Nottingham: 'I know you will be sorry to hear about Ball, but glad he is safe.'

The last five words had apparently been added as an afterthought, probably as the result of confidential information. Mr and Mrs Ball were inclined to accept the message, the more so for the reason that the War Office had informed them a day or so previously that no doubt direct news would come through to the military from those in the lines earlier than it could be furnished officially. Major-General Trenchard wrote on 14 May: 'I sincerely hope he is alive and well. I have received no further news yet, I am sorry to say.'

Two days later, the Under Secretary of State for War, answering a question in the House of Commons, said that the War Office had no further information as to the fate of Captain Ball.

Sir Henry Dalziel: 'Is there any ground for hoping that he is still alive?'

Mr Macpherson: 'We hope he is.'

On 20 May a statement was published in the Press that Alderman Ball had received official news that his son was a prisoner of war in Germany. This was not correct, and Alderman Ball still awaited the official confirmation which never came.

In the interval between the report of his disappearance and the confirmation of his death, there was a discussion in the House of Commons on the much-debated question whether or not more publicity should be given to the individual achievements of our airmen.

One member, Mr G. Terrell, suggested that there was no military object in suppressing the names of the pilots who, so far as he could see, were accomplishing deeds which had never been done before in the history of the world. 'We are told,' he said, 'that, with becoming modesty, they object to their names being mentioned ... It is due to the country that the action of these men should be publicly acknowledged.'

Mr Macpherson, in reply, said he had it on the authority of the general of the Royal Flying Corps himself,

> that the flying men feel that the men in the trenches have on many occasions to endure, unhonoured and unsung, the greatest hardships. They feel that it would be creating a distinction which they do not wish to see created, if they, on any individual occasion should be specially mentioned while those men are not ... The case which was brought to my notice by the hon. member for Kirkcaldy [Sir Henry Dalziel] was the case of a very gallant airman, Captain Ball. I have met Captain Ball. He would be the last person in the world to urge that this House should give him special preference over his gallant colleagues in the air service who have done very good work. Captain Ball, I think, has been responsible for over thirty machines. I remember when he came to see me with my hon. friend, one of the members for Nottingham, he was very modest. He was mentioned four times in despatches; I think he got the double bar to the D.S.O. and the Military Cross, and, if I remember aright, the War Office raised no objection at all to the very proper civic reception which was given by the city of Nottingham.

Captain Ball's name was again mentioned in the House on 16 May, when Mr Pemberton Billing asked whether the Under Secretary of State for War had any information as to the fate of

Captain Ball, and would he say what type of machine he was flying at the time he was reported missing.

Mr Macpherson: 'I am sorry to say that the War Office has no further information about the fate of this gallant officer. It is not considered desirable to mention the type of machine which he was using.'

Mr Billing: 'Is it not a fact that this officer requested continually not to be forced to cross the line on this particular type and design of machine; that when he brought down the forty-two German machines he was using a privately-designed machine, and that the first time he was sent over on this type he was lost?'

Mr Macpherson: 'I can scarcely believe that to be true, because I know this gallant officer never questioned any order given to him.'

Later, replying to Lord Henry Bentinck, as to whether Captain Ball refused to fly a particular machine, Major Baird said: 'I am much obliged to my noble friend for according me this opportunity of giving the most explicit denial to an allegation which is entirely without truth.'

From official sources, it was known what type of machine he was flying. When he went back to the front for the last time he asked if he could have a certain type of machine, as well as one of another make. Latterly he did not fly the first machine, and he asked for another of the second pattern, and told General Trenchard and his brother-pilots that once or twice he managed to get out of tight corners better with the second type. The names of these machines have not been disclosed for publication, but it is some satisfaction to know that in his last flight he was flying the machine of his choice.

CHAPTER 17

The Supreme Sacrifice

After a month of suspense, when inquiries were made by the International Red Cross Society, and in various other directions, the news came that Captain Ball was dead. The date on which he was reported missing was given as the date when he was killed also.

Major R. G. Bloomfield, his Squadron Commander, wrote:

> June 1st. It is with the greatest possible regret that I now have to inform you that messages have been dropped by the Germans stating that Captain Ball was killed on May 7th by a pilot of equal skill (believed to have been the German Baron Richthofen) and that he is buried at Annoeullin, in the north of Lens, in the locality in which his last fight took place.

A brother officer wrote:

> The German Flying Corps still retain some chivalry, and so one of their pilots risked crossing our lines in order that he might drop a message to the effect that Captain Ball had been 'killed in an air fight with an honourable opponent.' The message was enclosed in a metal cylinder.

The cylinder containing the little message was made of tin, painted black, about 8 inches in length, with a cork top, and is now in possession of the boy's father.

Included in the list of British aeroplanes that fell into German hands during May, published in the *North German Gazette*, was noted: 'three-decker, one-seater, No. 10,046: Captain Ball, dead.'

Information was obtained from German headquarters that Ball was killed in an air battle. The following is the translation of the telegram of 29 May sent to one acting on behalf of our prisoners of war: 'Captain Albert Ball, D.S.O., according to news received from Field Headquarters on the 15th May, has fallen on May 7th in an aerial fight. Details are unknown at Field Headquarters.'

It was learned that he was shot down at 8.30 p.m. by Lieutenant Freiherr von Richthofen. The Berliner *Tageblatt* announced that:

> The celebrated English aviator, Captain Albert Ball, who had brought down forty German aeroplanes and has been reported missing, was brought down in the course of an aerial combat with the Baron von Richthofen, Commandant of the crack German squadron which has brought down fifty-four adversaries.

Inquiries through the Frankfurt Red Cross as to whether he was shot dead or whether he was only wounded and died later in hospital, showed from what information was obtainable that he was killed outright and did not suffer. His machine was completely wrecked.

It seems that Ball was particularly desirous to fight a duel in the air with the famous Baron. Every day for a fortnight, according to one report, he flew over Richthofen's aerodrome and dropped cartels of challenge and defiance, inviting the German to come out and fight him, adding that he was waiting 'upstairs'. The challenge was not personally accepted. For although it was freely stated that it was the Baron who killed him it is surely evident that it was not a single-handed contest, but a fight against Richthofen and his squadron. The Baron, who has stated that he was the leader of the aerial 'circus,' which was 'ever scouring skies in search of British and French airmen,' himself gives the credit to his young brother.

This is the Baron's story:

My brother's twenty-second adversary was the famous Captain Ball, by far the best English flying man ... Captain Ball was flying a triplane and encountered my brother alone at the front.[1] Each one tried to grip the other, and neither exposed any vulnerable part. It proved a brief encounter. Neither of the two succeeded in getting behind the other.

Suddenly within a brief moment of mutual frontal attack both managed to fire some well-aimed shots. Both flew at one another; both fired. Each had a motor before him, and the chances of a hit were very slender, the speed being double as great as the normal. There was really little probability of either hitting the other.

My brother, who was somewhat lower, had banked his machine too much, and he lost his balance. For a few moments his machine was beyond control. Very soon, however, he regained command, but found that his opponent had shot both his petrol tanks to pieces. To land was therefore the only resource.

'Quickly! Out with the plug or the body will burn!' The next thought was, 'What has become of my opponent?' At the moment of canting he observed how the enemy also had swerved aside. He could therefore not be very far from him. The question arose: 'Is he over or under me?' He was below. My brother saw the triplane swerving again and falling over more steeply. Captain Ball fell and fell until he reached the ground. He was on our territory.

Both adversaries had in a brief moment of their encounter hit each other with their powerful machine-guns, and Captain Ball had received a shot in the head.

He had on him some photographs and newspaper cuttings from his home country in which he was greatly praised. He appeared shortly before to have been home on leave.

During Boelcke's time Captain Ball had destroyed thirty-six German machines. Now he, too, had met his master – or was it a coincidence that a great one such as he should also die the usual hero's death?

Captain Ball was without doubt the leader of the anti-Richthofen squadron, and I believe that now the Englishmen will prefer to abstain from trying to catch me.

But in spite of the Baron's tribute we know that Ball fell fighting against overwhelming odds. That was the opinion of our own airmen.

In lamenting his loss one would like to recall his own words: 'If anything should happen to me, as it quite easily may, I expect and wish you to take it well, for men tons better than me go in hundreds every day.'

Notes

1. The statements of those of his comrades who were with him shortly before his death clearly contradict the suggestion of a duel.

CHAPTER 18

'The Victoria Cross'

Two posthumous honours to this boy fighter of 'a hundred and fifty air battles,' were the Victoria Cross and the Croix de Chevalier de la Légion d'Honneur. It will be remembered that he had been previously decorated with the Military Cross, the Distinguished Service Order, with two bars, the Russian Order of St George, Fourth Class; and he was four times mentioned in despatches.

The following is the official description of the deeds for which he was awarded the VC:

For most conspicuous and consistent bravery from April 25th to May 6th, 1917, during which period Captain Ball took part in twenty-six combats in the air and destroyed eleven hostile aeroplanes, drove two down out of control, and forced several others to land.

In these combats Captain Ball, flying alone, on one occasion fought six hostile machines; twice he fought five, and once four. When leading two other British aeroplanes he attacked an enemy formation of eight. On each of these occasions he brought down at least one enemy.

Several times his aeroplane was badly damaged, once so seriously that but for the most delicate handling his machine would have collapsed, as nearly all the control wires had been shot away. On his returning with a damaged machine he had always to be restrained from immediately going out on another.

In all, Captain Ball has destroyed forty-three German aeroplanes and one balloon, and has always displayed most exceptional courage, determination and skill.

At the Investiture, on 21 July 1917, in the courtyard of Buckingham Palace, his Majesty the King presented the Victoria Cross to Mr and Mrs Ball. There was a rousing cheer from the crowd as the boy's parents came forward. The King told Mr Ball that his son had actually brought down forty-seven machines.

Later, Mr Ball received the following autographed letter from his Majesty:

> Buckingham Palace.
> It is a matter of sincere regret to me that the death of Lieutenant (temporary Captain) Albert Ball, D.S.O., M.C., Notts. and Derby Regiment and Royal Flying Corps, deprived me of the pride of personally conferring upon him the Victoria Cross, the greatest of all awards for valour and devotion to duty. [Signed, George, R.I.]

It would be as well to give here the official descriptions of Ball's achievements that were issued in connection with his other decorations.

Distinguished Service Order

For conspicuous gallantry and skill. Observing seven enemy machines in formation, he immediately attacked one of them and shot it down at fifteen yards' range. The remaining machines retired. Immediately afterwards, seeing five more hostile machines, he attacked one at about ten yards' range and shot it down, flames coming out of the fusilage. He then attacked another of the machines which had been firing at him, and shot it down into a village, where it landed on the top

King George V presenting Captain Ball's posthumous Victoria Cross to Mr and Mrs Ball at Buckingham Palace, 22 July 1917.

of a house. He then went to the nearest aerodrome for more ammunition, and returning, attacked three more machines, causing them to dive out of control. Being then short of petrol he came home. His own machine was badly shot about in this fight.

London Gazette, 26 September 1916.

Bar to the D.S.O.
For conspicuous skill and gallantry. When on escort duty to a bombing raid he saw four enemy machines in formation. He dived on to them, and broke up their formation, and then shot down the nearest one, which fell on its nose. He came down to about five hundred feet to make certain it was wrecked. On another occasion, observing twelve enemy machines in formation, he dived in among them, and fired a drum into the nearest machine, which went down out of control. Several more hostile machines then approached, and he fired three more drums at them, driving down another out of control. He then returned, crossing the lines at a low altitude, with his machine very much damaged.

London Gazette, 26 September 1916.

Second Bar to the D.S.O.
For conspicuous gallantry in action. He attacked three hostile machines and brought one down, displaying great courage and skill. He has brought down eight hostile machines in a short period, and has forced many others to land.

London Gazette, 25 November 1916.

The official description given when the Military Cross was awarded has been printed in a previous chapter.

How many machines did Ball bring down? The number given by the King – forty-seven – is probably the nearest correct total, but the actual number will never be known.

His record includes forty-one absolutely certain successes, ten moral certainties, and a large number of probabilities [said the *Morning Post*]. It is true that the list of leading German experts, whose 'scores' are published from time to time, includes the name of an air-fighter who is said to have made fifty, not out, to use a cricket phrase, but it is known that the German statisticians credit their men even with possibilities - to say nothing of probabilities - the idea being to persuade the German public that in war-flying, as in all other branches of modern warfare, their 'field greys' are more skilful and courageous than the best of their opponents. If his record were made up according to German notions of rigorous accuracy, Captain Ball would be credited with something like between eighty and ninety victories.

There were many occasions on which Ball would not go to the extent of collecting the evidence to prove the crashing of various machines which he and others felt absolutely certain must have been wrecked in the German lines.

It has been pointed out that the westerly and south-westerly winds so often prevailing on the western front often deprived our pilots of the necessary evidence as to crashed German machines. Ball made no mention at all of machines he knew to have been crashed, but had no corroborative evidence to offer.

On 10 June a memorial service was held at St Mary's Church, Nottingham. The procession, which was formed at the Exchange Hall, included the Mayor and Sheriff, Alderman Ball and his only surviving son (2nd Lieut. A. C. Ball), Captain I. M. Henderson, MC, RFC, representing his father, General Sir David Henderson, numerous officers, a detachment of the RFC, and representatives of the City Council and the other local bodies. The procession was headed by the City Police Band, and the processional route was lined by large crowds.

The parish church of Lenton, his birthplace, also held a memorial service.

The tributes to his memory that were published and spoken all over the world would fill a volume in themselves.

In addition to the letter from the King, already printed, Mr and Mrs Ball received the following from the King and Queen:

Buckingham Palace.

The King and Queen have learnt with deep regret of the death of your son, Captain A. Ball, whose conspicuous and consistent bravery won him the Victoria Cross.

Their Majesties deplore the loss of so gallant and distinguished an officer, and truly sympathise with you in your sorrow.

The procession leaving the Exchange and passing through the Market Place en route to St Mary's church, Nottingham, where the memorial service was held, 10 June 1917.

CHAPTER 19

World Tributes

> His blazing trail across the evening sky of Flanders, when he fell, was the most glorious funeral pyre that has fallen to the lot of mortal man. *Si Monumentum requeris.*

These were the words of the journal, *Aeronautics*, on the news of Capt. Ball's death.

It would be impossible to conclude this record of Captain Ball's life without giving some extracts from the letters and Press tributes that came from everywhere where there was enthusiasm for the cause of Britain and her Allies. His career and the manner of its ending made a striking appeal to the imagination of countless millions.

A Brigadier-General said: 'One of the bravest men I knew.'

From his Major-General: 'It was a tremendous blow to the R.F.C. ... He was given the Victoria Cross, and no man ever deserved it more than he did. I only wish he was alive to wear it.'

His Squadron Commander: 'I had hoped for the best all along, and the news of his death was a great shock to me, and will, I am afraid, be a great shock to all ...'

An Adjutant:

> Like everyone else in the Squadron, I loved him. He is missed and mourned by all his fellow officers and men. His record stands unsurpassed; as was said of another fearless warrior,

Little need to speak of Lancelot in his glory.
King, Duke, Earl, Baron –
Whom he smote he overthrew.

So with him; words are insufficient to pay tribute alike to his courage which was sublime and heroic, or to his skill which was that of the master craftsman.

I shall always remember the lovable and impulsive boy who was proud without being conceited and aware of his worth and merit without being ostentatious. So long as I live I shall feel the better for having known him, and I trust that the knowledge of what he accomplished for his country and of the fact that his home and fame will be for all time an example of unsurpassable courage.

A Captain in the RFC (who was with Captain Ball in his last flight) paid another tribute: 'He was always a very great man. I see they have given him the V.C. Of course, he won it a dozen times over – the whole squadron knows that.'

Another Officer wrote: 'He was absolutely worshipped out here as the flying man of the British Army.'

One of his comrades in the RFC said: 'Without doubt Ball was the bravest and boldest lad who ever wore wings.'

All the officers and men of the RFC mourned the loss of their idol – for such he undoubtedly was.

Another member of the Corps wrote to Mr Ball:

I am greatly upset, because I simply loved and adored Captain Ball, and would have gone through death for your son and my superior officer. He was so young, and it seems a shame Nottingham's son should die so young. England has lost her best aviator, but he died for his King and Country, and has died a warrior's death.

A Captain in the Royal Scots, BEF, wrote:

I saw young Ball at Vert Galland the day before he went amissing, and we had a great crack when we discovered that we were both O.T.'s, signifying old tridents of Trent College. He was a fine lad and his Major told me he thought no end of him. He had the chance of being at home, but he was a tiger for fighting, and, after all, he died the way he would most have liked to die.

A Captain in the Royal Fusiliers in East Africa, lying in hospital there, wrote:

I wish to pay my deepest homage, which surely every soldier and every Briton must owe him for ever. Such men – such angels or demi-gods, one might say – help us along a lot. How unspeakably proud his parents must be of him. God grant that such pride will help them to bear the loss of him a little easier, as also may the knowledge that every soldier must be sharing their sorrow and loss.

Letters and tokens of sympathy came from soldiers near and far. One came from Salonica glorying in the 'wonderful things he had done for his King and Country.' Another from a Sergeant in Egypt sympathising on the 'loss of England's greatest air-fighter, whose career has been followed with the keenest interest from England to the far East, and we fully realize the great loss of so brave a man.'

A famous airman – noted for his flights in the early days of aviation, and now engaged on important aeronautical work in this country – said: 'The gallant deeds of this noble and courageous boy will for ever be remembered.'

Tributes to his prowess and glory filled the columns of the Press. The following are typical selections:

'Beyond doubt his was the most wonderful series of victories yet achieved by a flying man of any nation.' – *Times*.

'Captain Ball's magnificent achievements in the air are among the most marvellous of the stirring deeds recorded for the war.' – *Pall Mall Gazette*.

'Britain's most famous airman.' – *Daily Express*.

'The wonderful airman.' – *Daily Sketch*.

'Greatest air record of the whole war.' – *Daily News*.

'The wonder boy of the Flying Corps.' – *Weekly Dispatch*.

'Such men as the ever memorable Captain Ball exhibit what Mr. Asquith, at the beginning of the war, called the "ancient and in-bred qualities of our race".' – *Daily Mirror*.

'Naturally, such a man was the idol of the Royal Flying Corps.' – *Star*.

'The marvellous young airman. One cannot help wondering why the authorities waited until he was dead before bestowing on him an honour which no man in the Army had more thoroughly earned.' – *Daily Chronicle*.

'He will be mourned by all England, indeed by a big part of the whole world, for his deeds were written of by the Press of all countries. To-day his name resounds throughout the land, and it will never be forgotten.' – *Manchester Guardian*.

'The most brilliant of British airmen.' – *Flying*.

'In many respects he was the English counterpart of the German flyer, Immelmann.' – *Flying*.

'Albert Ball was a king among men as he was a prince among flyers. Day after day he set out undaunted on his deadly errand, gambled his life, knowing full well the fate that lay in store for him, according to all human computation.' – *Aeronautics*.

'To a fallen hero. The name of Captain Albert Ball confers honour upon the Victoria Cross. His blazing trail across the evening sky of Flanders, when he fell, was the most glorious funeral pyre that has fallen to the lot of mortal man. *Si monumentum requeris*.' – *Aeronautics*.

'The loss of the King of British flyers, missing after his 44th victory, is unhappily true. Albert Ball was King of British aviation.' – *La Bataille*.

'The star of aviators.' – *Agence Havas*.

'His exploits are a tradition of the British Army.' – *Petit Parisian*.

'The super-airman, Captain Ball. His acts of bravery are countless. It is thus a great loss for the flying army of our Allies.' – *J'ai Vu*.

The French dependencies in Africa spoke in their newspapers of this 'Prodigy of prodigies, the glorious incognite of British aviation.' The Japanese Press referred in admiration to 'the leading British aviator' and his 'glorious record,' and the *Japan Advertiser* (Tokyo) reproduced at some length the report from the Havas Agency. The Portuguese Press reported sympathetically on the '*Morte dum aviador Ingles*,' and referred to him as '*O 'As' dos 'As' Inglezes*' – the 'Ace' of English 'Aces.' The Spanish newspapers commented on the '*Muerte de un aviador*,' and under the heading of '*El espritu deportive Ingles*.' From Switzerland came praise for the airman whose 'reputation for a brave and fearless flyer was world-known.'

The South American Press spoke with admiration of the '*heroe aviador, Captain Ball*,' and the world over praised his glorious life and death.

The Eccentric Club, London, has founded hostels for limbless men from the Army and Navy, homes where these wounded heroes are housed and cared for while being trained to earn their livelihood. One of the few hostels opened in London is known as 'The Captain Ball Hostel,' situated in King Edward's Road, Hackney, originated by his friend, Mr James White, and opened on 4 July 1917.

Brigadier-General Charlton, DSO, of the RFC, paid a glowing tribute to this man of heroic courage, and said that without doubt the splendid deeds which our airmen were now performing at the front were materially due to the example he set, and to the success which he achieved.

His native city decided that a statue should be erected 'in recognition of the distinguished services rendered by him to the Empire, as a member of the Royal Flying Corps, and as a token of the esteem and admiration of his fellow citizens and fellow countrymen.' Subscriptions have come from all classes, including soldiers all over the world.

'A brother pilot in France' enclosed a cheque 'from one who can appreciate to the full extent some of the many dangers and risks Captain Ball went through before he so gallantly gave his life for his country'; and another sent his tribute 'to the gallant youth whose brilliant work confers imperishable lustre on Nottingham.'

Referring to one of his comrades who had been killed in air-combat, Captain Ball once said when in Nottingham, 'I suppose they'll get us all sooner or later.'

And now Ball, and the object of his friendly rivalry, Captain Guynemer, have flown their last flight.

Captain Ball's valour has inspired others, not only in the Air Service but in other branches of the Army. How a battalion of Sherwood Foresters saved the day by rallying to the battle-cry of 'Remember, Captain Ball!' is worth recording here. The story is related by a Mansfield collier who was wounded while serving with the battalion:

> The Sherwoods took their plunge at the hottest part of the line, as usual [he said]. It was hot enough from the first moment we went over, but the further we went the hotter it became, until it seemed hot enough to raise blisters on a 5,000 year-old mummy. The place was swept by shell-fire, and machine- guns placed at intervals were keeping up a sort of cross-current of fire. The enemy thought they 'had us,' and got more daring. Fire outfits and more machine-guns played on us, and the Huns

even attempted a bayonet charge. We pretty soon let them see that that game wouldn't work, but that didn't alter the fact that we were making no headway so far as our real objective was concerned.

Then the young officer who was left in command of my company rose amid the storm of fire that was sweeping across towards us, and pointing to the enemy position called out: 'Remember Captain Ball, Sherwoods! It is up to you to avenge his death. Follow me!'

The thing electrified us. We seemed to forget all that had been worrying us, and we didn't wait to be called on to follow that brave officer of ours. We swept across the few score yards that separated us from where Fritz was hanging on in company of his machine-guns. The officer led us straight as a die for the first machine-gun, and in spite of the fact that he was under fire all the time he got at it and knocked out the crew himself. Then our company got into it, and we fairly did make the Germans pay for Captain Ball's death!

A charming memory is sent by an old comrade, Captain S. M. Wood, of the Military Aeronautics Directorate:

'Halloa, Ball! What are you doing with those tools?'

'Building a hut,' and he passed by.

'Who is that,' I asked.

'Our Ball,' was the reply, ' a magnificent youngster, as keen as possible on everything, fighting, flying, gardening, working, and yet always quiet, modest and charming – one of the best fellows that ever lived, and as brave as a lion.' That, in June, 1916, was the first time I saw Ball – the boy whom I learnt to admire and love with that strong affection that noble, chivalrous and brave men earn from their fellow men.

No man has ever before faced more dangers in a life's span than this man or boy faced in less than two years in France.

That Providence befriended him there is no doubt, but that his life was saved many times through that wonderfully balanced, clear, resourceful brain, through fortitude that has never been surpassed, we know, we who have worked with him and have watched him fighting and his home-coming, often with a thread (literally) between himself and death. He would land with his machine riddled with bullets, and go quietly, as was his way, to another machine and fly away in search of other enemy aeroplanes. After months of adoration in England he returned to France the same quiet, modest, unspoilt boy. To look at casually he appeared quite ordinary, and it was only when those dark piercing eyes would turn and rest on yours for a while that you realized that some strange power was there – some power that made him in some way different to other men.

Day after day he faced death so fearlessly, so nobly, that all men bore for him a great respect and a great love. He showed no unholy joy at the death of a foe – 'twas a foe fallen by his hand and killed for his country and his King that they may live. It was Duty, and England never had a son who served her more loyally, more truly and more bravely, and if Death were pleased and triumphant when he fell, she had great need to have pride in her victory, but triumphant she can never feel, for he, a mere child, faced her day after day, and if he feared her she knew it now and he knew that on the morrow he and she would meet again face to face – and yet he welcomed the morn that brought him to her presence.

His little greenhouse which he made in front of the hut which he had built himself, was carefully tended – no woman ever watched each plant more carefully. Yet no man ever knew his gun so well, or knew the strength of each nut and wire on his machine. No horseman knew the traits of the animal he rode and loved better than this boy knew the aeroplane he flew – he watched it and worked on it, and no detail was so small that it did not have his personal attention. The smallest neglect of detail might mean another 1 missing machine, and so loyalty and conscientiousness, with a natural desire for self- preservation, made him decide that only enemy shot or shell should rob the Empire of his services.

Then there are other well remembered pictures – his machine facing a target and his gun rattling merrily day after day, or his constant practice of manoeuvring and attack around the aerodrome, or in the air how he would dive out of a cloud and the sudden noise of his rotary machine heard above the roar of your stationary one would tell you that had he been an enemy you would have been falling to earth – a machine 'brought down.' It was practice for him and a warning to you of the necessity of constant alertness. His quiet 'I should have had you with the first burst,' when at the aerodrome again told you why his opponent and not he 'failed to return'. It was a comfort, too, to know that the watchful eye of the gallant lad with its sure aim was somewhere about to pick from off your tail any Huns that may have made life a little uncertain.

He was busy – always busy; and yet had time to tend his flowers, to improve his hut, to amuse his fellow officers with pleasing humour, and he had time to work, to fight and win.

Of his inner life, his eye was sure, his hand steady; for no vice had ever made his vision blurred or his hand shake, and he practised and worked, using to the utmost the gifts of God which he had not marred by evil thinking or living.

And if men talk of Nelson or Napoleon, of Kitchener, Stonewall Jackson and other great men with pride and often with love, shall we who fly and have flown, be forgiven if to us his name is not less sacred than theirs. He fought as well; none were more chivalrous than he and none lived more truly and cleanly. He led as well, and the most fearful of men would go and if needs be, die, if he were there to lead the way.

The others were men – tried and strong and middle-aged. He was but a child, a child for whom life held promise of great things, and so men believed in him, trusted him, and loved him well.

The Aero Club of America have decided to present a special War Medal to the family of the late Captain A. Ball, VC, DSO, as a tribute to the memory of England's foremost airman, the announcement to his father being couched in the following terms:

> The Aero Club of America recognising the glorious services rendered to the cause of the Allies by the heroic career of the late Captain Ball, V.C., through his indomitable courage and skill in the battles of the air, and who while in the performance of his patriotic duty, sacrificed his life for his country, wishes to add its tribute to his memory, by sending to his family the highest honour which is theirs to bestow – the special war medal of the Aero Club of America. This medal is being executed and struck in France, and as soon as it is ready will be forwarded to you by the Foreign Service Committee, which represents the Aero Club of America in France.

When the King visited France in July 1917, he was interested in the work of the Sherwood Foresters and Captain Ball's association with that regiment. His Majesty learnt that it was in sight of a battalion of his old regiment that the boy met his death.

The boy's grave is at Annoeullin, about five miles east of La Bassee. The Germans paid him homage. They buried him in the Cemetery of Honour, and they carved a laurel wreath upon the wooden cross which marks the grave.

Beneath the wreath are the words: 'HE GAVE HIS LIFE FOR HIS FATHERLAND.'

And so we come back to a simple memory of young Ball, the picture of the boy standing under the doorway of his old

school, and above, the inscription, 'England expects every man
to do his duty,' and the picture of his grave.

It is not many miles away from the great company of the
flower of the youth of our nation and our Empire who lie
buried at Vimy, Lens, Loos, Neuve Chapelle, and Ypres.

They are there with him – the pride of our race – tens of
thousands of them. They are the men of whom one of our
soldier poets has sung:

> We have given all things that were ours,
> So that our weeds might yet be flowers,
> We have covered half the earth with gore,
> That our houses might be homes once more;
> The sword Thou hast demanded, Lord;
> And now, behold the sword.[1]

This country will not forget the boy who, bareheaded with
his hair streaming in the wind, traversed the sky of Flanders
challenging his foes to battle. He was the first of the famous
airmen of the war whose names will forever be an inspiration
to the race.

The boys of the future England – an England that will
assuredly enjoy a greater peace, a greater freedom than the
world has yet known – will wonder at the simplicity and the
sacrifice of his life and the lives of his comrades.

They will marvel at the Albert Ball who could dig and sing
in his garden on the battlefield, and who sang above the clouds
because his heart was glad.

They will not be sorry that he did not rejoice at the death
of his foes, and will learn with pride of his chivalry and of his
love for, and devotion to his country, and, perhaps, they will
feel something of the poignancy of those words, 'I don't offer
because I want to go but because every boy who has loving
people and a good home should go out and stand up for it …'

We would end this volume with a passage from Albert Ball's favourite author – R. L. Stevenson:

... is there not something brave and spirited in such a termination? and does not life go down with a better grace, foaming in full body over a precipice, than miserably straggling to an end in sandy deltas? When the Greeks made their fine saying that those whom the Gods love die young, I cannot help believing that they had this sort of death in their eye. For, surely, at whatever age it overtakes the man this is to die young. Death has not been suffered to take so much as an illusion from his heart. In the hot-fit of life, a tip-toe on the highest point of being, he passes at a bound to the other side. The noise of the mallet and chisel is scarcely quenched, the trumpets are hardly done blowing, when, trailing with him clouds of glory, this happy-starred, full-blooded spirit shoots into the spiritual land.

Notes

1. Lieut. Geoffrey Howard.